COPIOUS HOSTING

A Theology of Access for People with Disabilities

Jennie Weiss Block

CONTINUUM
New York • London

2002

The Continuum International Publishing Group Inc
370 Lexington Avenue, New York, NY 10017

The Continuum International Publishing Group Ltd
The Tower Building, 11 York Road, London SE1 7NX

Printed in the United States of America

Library of Congress Cataloging-in-Publication Data

Block, Jennie Weiss.
    Copious hosting : a theology of access for people with disabilities / Jennie
Weiss Block.
        p.   cm.
    Includes bibliographical references.
    ISBN 0-8264-1349-8 (pbk.)
    1. Handicapped—Religious aspects—Christianity.   I. Title.
BT732.7 .B56   2002
261.8'324—dc21   2001054760

In memory of
Mary Beth Weiss
and
Bobby Bailey Weiss

~

Contents

PART III
A Theology of Access

Acknowledgments

I still have a little scrap of paper with a message my ten-year-old daughter took in October of 1998. In her best printing, she wrote, "Mr. Frank Oveis calling about your book" followed by a New York telephone number. She dutifully repeated the message to me when I called home from out of town, and then left the little piece of paper on my desk. Anyone who has children knows that the messages they take for their parents aren't always delivered on time. Neither are books, I have come to find out! Indeed, I am grateful that this project has been brought to fruition, and am aware that it would never have happened without the assistance and support of many people.

I owe the idea for this book to Stephen Happel, who suggested that the material from a lecture I presented to the faculty at the Weston Jesuit School of Theology would make a good book. Stephen, along with Nathan Mitchell, guided me expertly through the early stages of developing the concept for the book, and submitting the outline for publication.

This book reflects the knowledge, insights, and experience of many people in both the disability and theological fields. These people have been my teachers, colleagues, and conversation partners. They have listened, informed, challenged, critiqued, and supported me through the entire project. Many people have read different parts or all of my manuscripts at different stages, and have offered direction and comments that have been invaluable. Special thanks to Zoe DeBlasio and Katie Carroll, and others mentioned elsewhere in this acknowledgment, for a careful reading of the final draft.

I am grateful to my friends and colleagues in the disability field for their vision and commitment. I thank Joe Krieger and the Florida Disabilities Planning Council for many great assignments during my years as a consultant. I offer particular thanks to everyone at Sunrise Community, especially Les Leech, Kathy Whitaker, and Steve Weinger. I appreciate the many professional opportunities that I was given at Sunrise, and remember my years there as a very happy and fulfilling time.

Many thanks to the faculty and students in the Department of Theology and Philosophy at Barry University. Their willingness to teach theology to a middle-aged woman who didn't know eschatology from ecclesiology was generous beyond measure, and I will always be grateful for the opportunity to study theology in such a challenging and supportive atmosphere. Many of the graduate students that I have studied with over the last five years have been very helpful to me through conversation and feedback as I brought the topic of disability to theological reflection. Special thanks to all of my professors, especially Dr. Mary Jo Iozzio, Sister Veronica Koperski, Father John O'Grady, Dr. Alicia Marill, and Father John Markey, O.P., for their willingness to work with me as I explored the relationship between theology and disability over a variety of theological disciplines.

I offer grateful thanks to the Dominican friars in the Province of St. Martin de Porres for giving me a place in the church where my theological reflection could become a lived reality. The way they have shared their life with me has shaped my understanding of Christian hospitality. Special thanks to "my" Provincial, Alberto Rodriquez, O.P., and my good friends, Marcelo Solorzano, O.P., Wayne Cavalier, O.P., David Caron, O.P., and Hank Groover, O.P. It is surely fitting that the title of this book is taken from the work of the great Dominican theologian Edward Schillebeeckx, O.P.

A few special thanks are in order. My personal assistant, Lisa Manoogian, deserves recognition for her competency, calmness, and ability to keep things going on the home front which has allowed me time to think and to write. I am grateful to my editor, the esteemed Frank Oveis, for his confidence in this project, his patience with my slow progress, and his expert guidance through all phases. I will always be indebted to my theological mentor, Mark Wedig, O.P., for his wise direction, unrelenting demands on my intellectual development, and his willingness to befriend me. I am appreciative to Jorge Presmanes, O.P., for his ability and willingness to process almost any topic with insight and clarity, and especially for the comfort of his presence in my life. I am thankful for the support and devotion of my dear friend, Scott O'Brien, O.P., who has taught me to understand and be able to write of friendship as communion.

I am blessed with a wonderful family and the best of friends who have supported me in a variety of ways including helping me with many other priorities in my busy life, never complaining about my lack of availability, and most especially for showering me with God's love and mercy. My life-long friend, Father Jerry Devore, has been a spiritual presence in the life of our family for over three decades. Special thanks to my sister, Laurie Nuell, for tangibly supporting me in everything I undertake, and for being the sister everyone dreams of having. My father, Jay Weiss, has been the perfect role model for generosity and hospitality throughout my entire life, and his unwavering confidence in me means as much to me in my adulthood as it did in my childhood. My mother, Mary Beth Weiss, and my husband, Sandy Block, continue to inspire me in death, as they did in life. Finally, I thank my three fine children, Christopher Barat, Mary Elizabeth, and Genevieve Laurette. They have been such good teens that I have had the energy and presence of mind to write a book; and they bring me, on a daily basis, the greatest of joy and pleasure.

This brings copious thanks to all of you along with my enduring appreciation and love.

Introduction

*The whole community welcomes you with love and stands ready
to help you.*

Rite of Christian Initiation of Adults, 1972

The general purpose of this book is twofold. First, to forge a
"conversation" between "disability" and "Christianity," and
second, to allow the insights and reflections from this conversation to guide the development of a theology of access that en-
sures people with disabilities take their rightful place within the
Christian community. This book is intended primarily for two
audiences: pastoral ministers, theologians, and students of theology who are interested in understanding the experiences of
people with disabilities, and who seek to create a welcoming
place and space for people with disabilities within the Christian
community; and people with disabilities who are interested in
exploring the relationship between disability and Christianity,
and for whom the sacred mysteries hold meaning.

Human Experience as Source of Revelation:
My Own Story

The great German theologian Karl Rahner believed that ordinary
everyday living is filled with experiences of God's presence and

grace. He considered mysticism, the hidden experience of transcendence and the discovery of God in all things, to be available to everyone.[1] The great American theologian David Tracy claims that for contemporary theological investigation to be relevant it must depend on two principle sources: Christian texts and common human experience and language.[2] These two seemingly separate ideas—the mysticism of everyday life, and a reliance on common human experience and language in the theological endeavor—have made clear to me the integral relationship between theology and life. In particular, my understanding of disability and my experiences with people with disabilities have been a source of revelation. I begin with a short account of my personal background, which I hope will explain why this is so, as well as give the reader some sense of who I am and my philosophy and politics of disability. I am not a person with a disability and I do not speak for people with disabilities. They are quite capable of speaking for themselves and are best able to articulate their personal and individual experiences. I am a "secondary consumer," an expression used in the disability field to indicate a person who has a family member who has a disability. I come to reflection on the topic of disability because of my life experiences as a family member of a person with multiple disabilities, a friend of many people with disabilities, and a disability professional for eighteen years. At one level, I speak reluctantly for I believe it is essential that people with disabilities take the lead and speak of their own experiences. At another level, I believe that my perspective is valuable and worth sharing; however, I speak only for myself.

I am a white, middle-aged, middle-class, Roman Catholic woman. I was widowed in 1991 and am engaged in the entertaining process of guiding my three fine children through the teen years to adulthood. I am the oldest of eight children, five of whom were adopted by my extraordinary parents. The youngest of my siblings, Bobby, was adopted when he was four years old. Our whole family adored Bobby and was devoted to him. My sister met him while doing volunteer work in high school and brought him home on the Fourth of July for the afternoon. The only word he knew how to say was "Mommy." However, this one word served him well and probably changed the course of his lonely, young life, because using what we later learned was his keen intuition and judgment of people, he immediately began to call our mother "Mommy." He started coming over on the weekends to visit, and when he arrived with bruises on his face and back in the shape of handprints, my Mother cried, and refused to send him back. We knew he was mentally retarded, had many physical disabilities, and had been abandoned and subjected to extreme mental and physical abuse in the first four years of his life. His psychiatrist told us he had experienced more traumas in four years of life than most adults will ever experience. He had several serious medical conditions, terrible behavior and emotional problems, and a certain charm that transcended all of his problems. We were given lots of incorrect information and unwanted advice. We were told that Bobby would be a dwarf (wrong, he grew to be 5'9") and that he would never learn to speak (wrong again, and when he did begin speaking his "colorful" vocabulary gave us some indication about the places he had lived and what he had been called). Agency social workers took bets on how long "the beautiful, blond lady in the big white house would keep the bad, little boy." One doctor told my mother, in front of Bobby, that there was nothing that could be done for him, and that she should get rid of him as soon as possible. She bundled him up, carried him out of there, and found another doctor.

In 1974, when Bobby was twelve, and I was twenty-eight, our mother died, after a long and terrible illness, just six months short of her fifty-second birthday. Her last words to me were, "Take care of Bobby." I kept my promise, and until Bobby died thirteen years later, I was one of his primary caretakers. I learned to be an advocate the hard way: trying to find services, schools, and knowledgeable and caring medical personnel for Bobby. Even with adequate financial resources and my tenacious personality, I was often overwhelmed and depressed. The lack of

services and programs, the blatant discrimination, the misunder-
standings about what disability is, the ignorant fears of others
("No, it's not contagious"), the stares and mean comments, the
downcast eyes and pitying glances—all had made me aware of
the pervasive oppression that permeates the lives of people with
disabilities.

In 1979, I responded to a "call" of sorts to go and work in the
disability field. It was difficult to leave my administrative job at
Carrollton School of the Sacred Heart where I was surrounded
by hope and beauty, but I knew I had to go. For the next sixteen
years, I pursued many avenues of service: administration, policy and organizational development, national conference planning, grant writing, project development and management,
legislative advocacy, and staff training and education. My work
was intense, frustrating, and rewarding. The disability field is
not glamorous. I was appalled by the terrible injustices I encountered. I was naively shocked by the lack of funding, programs, and services that were available. I was horrified to learn
that many people with disabilities had no job, no home, no
friends—all the things I took for granted. My work allowed me
to see first-hand how people with disabilities are perceived and
treated.

Our family did everything we could to make sure my brother
had a good life. I think I was a good advocate for him. There
were many hard decisions along the way. Even though he had
a terrible temper and inappropriate outbursts, even though he
limped and looked different, even though he couldn't read and
had a limited vocabulary, we chose to let him make his way in
his world. Well-meaning friends and smart professionals questioned our judgment and advised us to wait until he was older
and, one hoped, better behaved and less likely to fail. We ignored
them, believing in what Bob Perske calls "the dignity of risk."[3]
Bobby had limited academic success so we looked for other
ways for him to succeed. He became a champion swimmer, and
a great dancer, and he had an appealing personality that he
learned to use to his advantage. At first our family friends became his circle of friends, but we wanted him to have friends his

own age and friendships that he established on his own. Against the advice of almost everyone, we let him go to a large inner-city high school with a decent special education program where, because of the enlightened attitude of a great school principal, he would have the opportunity to attend some classes with nondisabled kids. Initially his friends were from his special education class, but he soon became friends with a very unlikely group of inner-city kids. His relationship with them was a perfect testimony to the mystery of friendship. My brother's friends were mostly African-Americans, tough, street smart, and independent. He was white, rather spoiled, and mentally retarded. They put up with none of his nonsense (and did more to curb his temper outbursts than ten years of behavior management programs!). He provided them the opportunity to expose their vulnerable side. In some unexplainable way, it worked. I will always remember that he joined them at the senior prom, where dressed in a tacky tuxedo, surrounded by his friends, he danced the night away. He told me he was the best dancer there.

Bobby's kidneys failed on his nineteenth birthday, and he was very sick for three years before he died on June 7, 1987. Many of his friends, some we didn't even know, came to his funeral to say good-bye to him and tell us how much they loved him. Throughout my career, I have lectured on disability all over the country. After talking about things like service models, political trends, funding formulas, and community inclusion, I always mention my brother. I say that if we had waited until he was older, or better behaved, or "ready" to go out into the world, he would never have known what it is to have a friend and be a friend. I say this during my lectures, and I mention it now, because I believe that access and inclusion are urgent matters.

The Case for a Disability Theology of Access

In 1995, I made the difficult decision to leave my work in the disability field to pursue a master's degree in theology, fulfilling a long-held personal dream. I thought that I was leaving the disability field and bid a tearful good-bye to my friends and colleagues. However, I was drawn back to disability at the urging of some of my professors who wisely advised me to "write about what you know about"; hence, I began to consider disability in relation to theology. My work in this area has convinced me that there is a great need for disability theology. To my knowledge, this has not been done in any systematic way. While there is extensive material on disability in the medical, psychological, sociological, and clinical fields, there is surprising little on religion and disability. Considering the fact that there are approximately fifty-four million people in the United States with some type of physical or mental disability, this is significant and telling. Much of what has been written has either a spiritual or pastoral orientation and is written without an awareness of the new paradigms in the disability field. Much of what exists is not written by people with disabilities or has been written without direct consultation and input from people with disabilities. As I began to explore this topic, I became aware that, with few exceptions, the theological community is unaware of the radical new vision of disability emerging in this country.

I want to make the important point that I am in no way ignoring or minimizing the significant emphasis that has been placed on the inclusion of people with disabilities in many religious denominations in the past twenty-five years. Major efforts and resources have been expended and have succeeded in accomplishing a great deal within the Christian community for people with disabilities, particularly in the pastoral area. In my own Roman Catholic tradition, we have a national office for persons with disabilities (NCPD) headed by long-time disability rights activist Mary Jane Owen. The Catholic bishops have issued several pastoral letters on the inclusion of people with disabilities and many dioceses have local disability offices. I am familiar with some of the work that is being done in the Episcopal Church, Lutheran Churches, the National Council of Churches, and in the Jewish community, and I know that many other congregations have also turned their attention to the inclusion of people with disabilities. A Bibliography and Resource List with information about many of these resources, as well as a listing of spiritual and theological books on this subject, are included at the end of this book. Nonetheless, since I began to study theology in 1995 and became actively engaged in the religious and theological communities, I have again and again encountered theologians, and pastoral ministers, both ordained and non-ordained, who are not aware or do not understand that there have been major paradigm shifts in philosophy and practice related to the disability community.

It is a reality that the world in which the Christian community exists is pluralistic and secular. Christianity, no longer the dominant culture, is impacted and influenced by the events of the wider society. The feminist movement in the wider society was the precursor of the feminist movement in theology. If Simone de Beauvoir had not written *The Second Sex*, Elisabeth Schüssler Fiorenza would not have written *In Memory of Her: A Feminist Theological Reconstruction of Christian Origins*. For contemporary theological reflection to have meaning it must intersect with the secular, pluralistic world. In contemporary American society, people with disabilities are part of both a civil rights movement with radical new paradigms and an emerging disability culture. The philosophy that drives the disability movement is explained in detail in chapter 5. It can be summed in this way: people with disabilities are saying that there is nothing wrong with being disabled, and "that there is no pity or tragedy in disability and that it is society's myths, fears and stereotypes that most make being disabled difficult."[4] As Nancy Mairs puts it, "A great many people with disabilities like their lives a lot. I happen to be one of them. We tend to repudiate the medical model of disability, which views us as sick and in need of a cure, and the mechanical model, in which we are broken and require repair."[5] People with disabilities do not want sympathy or pity but instead are demanding equality, independence, dignity, and full inclusion in all areas of life. The influence of this movement and culture, whether consciously or unconsciously, has created a particular context and identity for people with disabilities and for their families and friends. In order to be relevant and to avoid patronization, any attempt to theologize about the experience of being disabled or to minister to people with disabilities must be informed by an understanding of the thinking that shapes the disability rights movement. Just as it would be both demeaning and impossible to theologize about or minister to the Cuban-American people without an understanding of their self-articulated experience of political exile, it is likewise demeaning and impossible to theologize about or minister to people with disabilities without understanding the experience and culture from which they come.

My personal experiences prompted me to ask many hard theological questions. What is the Christian understanding of disability? What should it be? Does the theological community's understanding of the disabled person need to be challenged? In what way have common interpretations of the disability Scripture passages contributed to the oppression of people with disabilities? How do the common perceptions about disability in the Christian tradition contrast with the philosophical concepts of the disability movement? Are these concepts compatible with the basic tenets of life within the Christian community? Do people with disabilities need a critical liberation theology of disability? And most importantly, how can the Christian community provide greater access to people with disabilities?

This book is an attempt to answer these and other related questions, and to facilitate a conversation between the Christian community and people with disabilities. Is it possible for the Christian community and people who have been shaped by the contemporary disability movement to enter into conversation with each other? Or is the foundational thinking of each group so much at odds that meaningful conversation is impossible? As a disability advocate and a theologian, the answer to this question has dominated my thinking on the topic about which I write, indeed, it has slowed down the publication of this book by two years! The disability movement is the product of the democratic liberalism of the Enlightenment based on a political philosophy that values equality, independence, and individual rights. Christianity is a two-thousand-year-old tradition that values the community over the individual, interprets life through ritual and symbol, and believes suffering can be transformative. Where does the strident language of civil rights find a home in Christian theology? Are there ways to interpret the Scriptures and Christian symbols that will resonate within the disability community and support the progress toward inclusion that people with disabilities have made in the wider society? To date, attempts at this conversation have been rocky. In an article entitled "Barriers and Bridges: Relating the Disability Rights Movement and Religious Organizations," Nancy Eiesland writes of "the distant and sometimes tense relationship between the leadership of the disability rights movement and religious organizations, including many of those commissioned to service people with disabilities."[6] She notes that while good working relationships, personal friendships, and fruitful coalitions do exist, difficult or cool relationships are relatively widespread, especially among the leadership.[7] The historical and ideological reasons for this conflict are explained in part I of this book.

In spite of these differences, I remain hopeful that a meaningful conversation is possible. I suggest two possible approaches to facilitate this exchange. The first approach, which is the primary methodology used in this book, is called a "critical correlation."

This methodology, developed by David Tracy in *Blessed Rage for Order*, is a revisionist model. It is committed to what Tracy believes is the central task of contemporary Christian theology: "the dramatic confrontation, the mutual illuminations and corrections, the possible basic reconciliation between the principal values, cognitive claims, and existential faiths of both a reinterpreted post-modern consciousness and a reinterpreted Christianity."[8] Tracy's thesis is that the two principle sources for theology are Christian texts and common human experience and language. He claims that the contemporary theological task involves a critical correlation of the results of the investigation of these two sources.[9] The investigation of these sources takes an "historical and hermeneutical approach"[10] and understands the "texts" to include the major expressions of the Christian tradition while recognizing that human experience and language have a religious dimension. In other words, in this case, the experience of disability has religious meaning, and therefore can be brought into "conversation" with the "texts" of the Christian tradition. The final step in the critical correlation is for the theologian to bring this conversation between disability and Christianity to theological reflection.

To attempt a critical correlation of disability and Christianity is a hard task. There is no doubt that some of the "texts" and "language" of both groups will be foreign and perhaps even threatening to each other. Interpreting disability as a religious, spiritual, and theological reality and seeking what Eiesland calls the "moral meaning of disability"[11] have the potential of being highly provocative to both groups. The theological community must learn about the philosophy that drives the disability movement and, then, be willing to critique the Christian tradition in light of that philosophy. In like fashion, the disability community must be willing to search the Christian tradition for ways that can give meaning to the experience of being disabled. As stated earlier, a critical correlation between Christianity and disability is a complex and difficult project. On some points, disagreement is inevitable. But try we must, for it is not possible for inclusion to occur in isolation.

Another approach that might be taken to facilitate this conversation is the development of a critical liberation theology of disability. This approach has merit because liberation theologies are the primary place in Christian theology where social justice and civil rights converge. However, in order to develop a critical liberation theology, a significant methodological shift is necessary because the primary hermeneutical key in liberation theologies is oppression. I believe, at least at this point, it is best to begin the conversation using a critical correlation for it permits a two-sided conversation with a broader focus. A discussion of the advantages and disadvantages of a critical liberation theology of disability is sketched out in chapter 6 of this book.

An Overview of the Book

This book has three primary tasks and is organized in three corresponding parts. The first task is to explain the philosophical concepts of the disability movement to the theological community. In part I, I describe the social location of disability beginning with general and statistical information about the worldwide disability community. Next, I reflect on the central issues surrounding disability that reveal the social and cultural constructions, as well as the paradox and ambiguity embedded in this topic. Next, the experiences of people with disabilities are explored by considering the perceptions and stereotypes that perpetuate the oppression of people with disabilities. An overview of the key legislation, people, and events of the disability movement and a description of the philosophical concepts of the movement are offered along with an overview of the Americans with Disabilities Act. This section closes with a discussion on the emerging disability culture and its potential relationship to Christianity.

The second task of this book is to examine the Christian tradition from a disability perspective. Part II begins with a look at key theological topics such as Christian anthropology, embodiment, spirituality, and social justice including a discussion on the possible need for a critical liberation theology of disability. The next chapter critiques three of the major expressions of the Christian tradition: Scripture, liturgical worship, and sacramental access. This section concludes with a discussion on the purpose of a theology of access and the challenges and limits of access and inclusion.

The third task of this book is to present a theology of access for people with disabilities. Grounded in the insights in parts I and II, part III develops a disability theology of access with a supporting Christology, pneumatology, and ecclesiology, all of which include concrete suggestions on how to create an accessible environment that welcomes people with disabilities. The book ends with a proposal for a spirituality of disability based in friendship and shared vulnerability.

Guiding Principles

Four fundamental principles guide the development of my work. First, people with disabilities share fully in human nature and are not in any way inferior to people who are not disabled. Second, to reflect on disability is to reflect on the mystery of God's love and the great paradoxes of the Christian message. Third, people with disabilities are oppressed, and the Christian community has an obligation to respond to this injustice by challenging the structures and perceptions, including their own, that are oppressive, and by making changes that lead to full access and inclusion for people with disabilities. And finally, I hold that the mandate for access and inclusion is biblically based, central to our baptismal promise and commitment, and rooted in the Triune God. My work acknowledges that human experience is an essential and valid starting point, and that lived experience is revelatory. It is my intention that this book be both theoretical and practical; in other words, intended to make you both think and act, for I am absolutely certain that the time to welcome others into the Body of Christ is now.

I hope that bringing disability issues to theological reflection is an idea whose time has come and that this book will be one beginning of a fruitful conversation about the multivalent connections and relationships between disability and theology. Moral theologian and Thomistic scholar James Keenan, S.J., claims that one of the reasons that it is important to continue to study the thirteenth-century theologian Thomas Aquinas today is because Thomas "draws us into the habit of inquiring deeply."[12] This is what is asked of the reader of this book: to set aside preconceived ideas about disability and inquire deeply into this demanding and paradoxical topic. I hope that I can convince you that creating access is a mystical and moral matter, and ultimately becomes the real test of whether, in light of our baptismal promise "to welcome with love and stand ready to help," we can, with integrity, self-identify as the Christian community.

PART I

THE CONTEMPORARY
DISABILITY MOVEMENT

O N E

~

People with Disabilities

*[I]t is mistaking the diversity of persons with disabilities to expect
or desire that they all have the same view or values. Some are Yan-
kee fans, other favor the Mets; some are men, others women; some
are black, others white; many are poor but some affluent; some
politically liberal, some conservative; some see gains won primarily from individual efforts, others from group action.*

Alan Gartner and Tom Joe
Images of the Disabled, Disabling Images[1]

Depending upon the definition used, it is estimated that there
are between forty-three and forty-nine million Americans with
one or more physical and/or mental disabilities[2] making people
with disabilities the largest minority in the country, the next
largest being the Hispanic/Latino community, followed by the
African-American community. Over five hundred million people worldwide have a disabling condition, ten percent of the
world population.[3] These numbers are increasing as the population as a whole grows older.

There are literally hundreds of different types of disabilities
with varying degrees of involvement. About fifteen percent of

people with disabilities are born with their disability; the rest become disabled at some time during their life usually as a result of illness or accident. Some disabilities are permanent; others are temporary. There are people with developmental disabilities such as mental retardation, physical disabilities such as paraplegia, and mental disabilities and sensory disabilities such as blindness or deafness. Many people have multiple disabilities. Some disabilities, like epilepsy, are hidden. Some disabilities are static, such as the loss of a hand or leg. Some are episodic, such as seizure disorders. Some are progressive, such as muscular dystrophy. Some are progressive and unpredictable, such as multiple sclerosis. Obesity and stuttering are included by some as disabilities, and the Americans with Disabilities Act protects people with AIDS and HIV. Many people with disabilities attempt to "pass" and choose not to self-identify as disabled. In other words, they hide their disability to avoid the stigma of being labeled. This creates considerable tension, from the worry of being discovered, and limits their ability to seek assistance and support.

Unlike gender, race, national origin, and sexual orientation, one can join the ranks of "the disabled" at a moment's notice. One can also have "double membership" and be an African-American, or a woman, or gay as well as disabled, which can change and impact the experience of being disabled. For example, feminists often write of disabled women being treated differently than disabled men.[4] "Disability knows no socioeconomic boundaries," notes Patrisha Wright, the Washington lobbyist for the Disability Rights Education and Defense Fund. "You can become disabled from your mother's poor nutrition or from falling off your polo pony."[5] A person who is disabled from birth or from childhood generally has a very different experience and social context than a person who becomes disabled as an adult.

The disability movement could be named as the prototype movement of postmodernity. It has several distinctive characteristics. It is a relatively quiet, hidden movement. Unlike other civil rights movements, there are no highly visible leaders. Even with the passage of the Americans with Disabilities Act, in contrast to gay rights or women's rights, the disability agenda is not well known. A defining characteristic is radical pluralism. Joseph Shapiro calls it a "mosaic movement" for the 1990s with diversity as its central characteristic.[6] People with disabilities will express many perspectives depending upon the nature of their disability, their age, sex, socioeconomic situation, values, and life experiences. There is no "disabled person's perspective." Inherent in this diversity is considerable tension. This tension is often related to issues of resource allocation, status, and even the desire to distance oneself from people with certain types of disabilities. In a sense, there are many strands or mini-movements within the larger movement, which are usually defined by issues related to a particular type of disability. For example, people with mental retardation and their families are concerned with institutional closure, while people with severe physical disabilities are interested in attendant services.

This book uses what is known in the disability field as a "disability-neutral" or "cross-disability" approach that refers to all people with disabilities, making no distinction between types of disability. Often, for understandable reasons, writing and research are focused on a particular subgroup within the disability community. For example, in *The Disabled God*, Nancy Eiesland is clear when she says, "In this work, the designation 'persons with disabilities' will refer to persons with physical disabilities only."[7] Certainly there are instances when focusing on a subgroup can be justified as practical; however, using a disability-neutral approach is desirable whenever possible as distinctions often lead the most vulnerable people to further stigmatization.

Another distinctive feature of the disability movement is that a large percentage of those actively involved in the movement are nondisabled people, usually family and friends of the person with a disability or dedicated professionals. While the large number of both nondisabled people and professionals can be problematic, particularly if disabled persons are not allowed to speak and act on their own behalf; overall, however, I think the result of this broad coalition has ultimately been helpful for it has brought many powerful people into the movement, and has been less isolating for people with disabilities. Consider how different the gay and lesbian rights movement would be if half the people in the movement were straight.

The disability community is the only minority group with a huge social service system. There are literally hundreds of different types of programs, organizations, and agencies on the local, state, and federal level that assist people with disabilities. These are funded by state and federal monies, as well as by local communities. Vast amounts of money are spent on disability programs operated by both the public and private sectors. This is, in a sense, where one finds the best and worst of disability. In the past twenty years, I have seen agencies and programs that are so horrible that they haunt me still. People with disabilities tell terrible stories of bungling bureaucracy, humiliation, and loss of personal control and decision making. On the other hand, I have seen agencies and programs that stand for everything good and facilitate greatly improved lives for people with disabilities and their families. There are also many related careers in the disability field: physical therapists, occupational therapists, personal attendants, direct-care workers, social workers, program directors, employment specialists, job coaches, to name just a few. Many of the people that work in the disability field have chosen this work because of personal or family experiences.

Another distinctive feature of the disability movement is that there are many people who are quite vulnerable, who are unable to speak for themselves, or who need complete physical assistance. I spent several years in my early career working for an agency that provided assistance and support to people with profound and severe mental retardation. Many had been abandoned by their families and were dependent on the welfare system and the kindness of strangers. During my years of conference planning, I assisted many people with physical disabilities who required full-time attendant care for toileting, bathing, dressing, eating, and other daily functions. These people are central to the integrity of the disability movement, and it is critical that their existence and their needs are not hidden, disguised, or ignored.

Marked by radical pluralism, this quiet civil rights movement is powerful, intense, and dynamic. Upon careful thought, one realizes that disability is complex and multifaceted. Many contemporary moral, ethical, and religious issues such as poverty and economic injustice, public policy, employment, health care and allocation of medical resources, education, biomedical ethics, and feminism intersect with disabilities. There are Christological, ecclesiological, pneumatological, and spiritual implications. Reflection on the discrete reality we call "disability" raises profound and age-old questions relating to suffering, the plight of those marginalized by society, and the dramatic themes of oppression, liberation, justice, and transformation. As we move to consider what a disability is and attempt to define who is disabled, we are confronted with contradiction and ambiguity.

TWO

~

Defining Disability

Christmas 1977, I was 18 years old, independent and grown-up, working on a sheep ranch in Australia. Two years later, I spent Christmas in the hospital, my body drained of movement. I had broken my neck in a diving accident on Labor Day. How could God give me both of these Christmases in one lifetime? The mystery, paradox, and contradictions of faith and God's appetite for incongruity pull me as nothing else does.[8]

Edward B. Bennett, III
Student at Yale Divinity School

What Is a Disability? Who Is Disabled?

These are complicated questions filled with contradiction and ambiguity. Any effort to define disability or to name an individual as disabled is laden with normative claims, legal considerations, and functional measures. Statisticians have a difficult time agreeing on the number of people who have a disability because there is no single definition of what constitutes a disability. Is it physical in nature? Is it socially constructed? Is it related to the ability to perform activities? How can degrees of disability be measured? Many theories attempt to explain what a disability is and what it means to be disabled. Beyond the clinical definitions of particular disabling conditions, is it possible to define what disability actually is? A number of definitions and perspectives are offered demonstrating the range of thought on this question.

Susan Wendell, in her article, "Towards a Feminist Theory of Disability," says a disability is "socially constructed from a biological reality."[9] This definition acknowledges the power that dominant cultural norms have in shaping the perceptions we have of people with disabilities and what it means to be disabled. If eyeglasses and contact lenses had not been invented or were not culturally normative, most middle-aged people would find their ability to see and to read and write greatly limited. They would have a disability that was socially constructed from a biological reality.

Under the Americans with Disabilities Act of 1990 a disability is defined as (a) a "physical or mental impairment that substantially limits one or more of the major life activities of an individual; (b) a record of such an impairment; or (c) being regarded as having such an impairment."[10] This is a broad definition focusing on life activities in relation to limitation. It is significant in that it acknowledges the power of perception in defining disability. As this definition is tied to national civil rights legislation, it is subject to legal interpretation.

Al Condeluci expresses another view in his book *Interdependence: The Route to Community.* Quoting Frank Bowe in *Handicapping America*, he states: "The concept that handicaps result from interactions between disabilities and environments is well illustrated in primitive cultures; survival depends upon strength and agility, so physical disabilities become handicapping." Condeluci adds: "In this perspective, one is only handicapped when the interaction between the individual and the environment is interrupted. If something can augment the interruption; the handicap would be removed."[11] This definition locates disability within a functional context and focuses on the ability to accomplish tasks.

Attempts to name and describe disability often reflect the philosophical position of the individual suggesting the concept. Can we name with certainty who is disabled? It is clear that no singular definition is conclusive. Susan Wendall argues that "failure to recognize the standards of structure, function, and ability are socially relative could be dangerous to people with disabilities." Therefore an individual who might be considered disabled in one setting would not be described as disabled in another setting.[12] She recognizes the possibility that the primary causes of a disabled person's inability to do certain things may be social; from lack of opportunities, lack of accessibility, lack of services, poverty, or discrimination.[13] Thus, an inability to articulate a definition with certainty and clarity remains. However, if we are to grapple with complex philosophical and practical issues related to disability, we must continue to consider the multivalent meanings of these definitions. As we consider this evasive question, we will find our definition subject to fluidity and change that lead to reflection on related questions.

Are We All Disabled?

Many propose the idea that we are all disabled, just in different ways. While it may be true that we all share experiences of limitation, the particular experience of people with disabilities should not be ignored or relativized. Charles Gourney expresses his opinion in this way:

> Some well-meaning theologians have addressed this issue but unfortunately not always in a helpful manner. They say that disability is relative, that we are all disabled to some degree even if we do not think of ourselves that way: I have an ache here and a pain there. I get a stomachache every Thursday afternoon, I have a rotten temper, I'm bald, I have a terrible singing voice. Every-

one is disabled, so we should not judge anyone. While well-intentioned, this attitude sweeps under the rug some very real problems that people with disabilities must face. It may be true that no one has a perfect body, and that many of these imperfections are genuine inconveniences, but they do not usually reach the point where one feels and is excluded by mainstream society. This is one crucial difference between being disabled and physically imperfect.[14]

Barbara J. Blodgett, in her article "Graced Vulnerability," says, "This is not to imply that we are all in some way 'disabled.' Disabilities are discrete conditions that, because of the way they get defined socially, mean suffering and oppression for certain people."[15]

Others claim that there is no such thing as a disability. If all disability is socially constructed or if we are all disabled, then no one is disabled. In his article "Deaf is Beautiful," Andrew Solomon says,

> It is tempting, in the end, to say there is no such thing as a disability. Equally, one might admit that almost everything is a disability. There are as many arguments for correcting everything as there are for correcting nothing. Perhaps it would be most accurate to say that "disability" and "culture" are really a matter of degree. Being deaf is a disability and a culture in modern America; so is being gay; so is being female; so even increasingly is being a straight white male. So is being paraplegic, or having Down syndrome.[16]

The same problem is associated with both theories. Both discount the difficulties experienced by people with disabling conditions. It is not easy to be disabled in a world that is designed for nondisabled people. People with disabilities cope with particular problems that are not experienced by nondisabled people, and we do them an injustice by not recognizing and attempting to understand their uncommon situations.

And yet, Dennis Schurter makes the point that "Finally, we

dare not exclude ourselves from the family of those who have disabilities, for then we are at risk of excluding ourselves from the kingdom of God, as did the Pharisees of old. We each have our own physical, emotional, and spiritual limitations. It is only when we recognize our own needs that we can be open to receive God's healing power in our own lives."[17] Let there be no doubt that our support for those who are people with disabilities and the acceptance of the explicit reality of our own limitations are not mutually exclusive activities but are, in fact, deeply related and connected.

Perhaps, in the end, it is best for all people, disabled and nondisabled alike, to acknowledge that our solidarity is found in the sharing of the human condition from which no one is excluded. Our unity can be found in our common, but different experiences of joy, pain, peace, loss, hope, limitation, and suffering, and in our shared dependency on God's love and mercy.

What Are We Afraid Of?

I once did a presentation on disability to a group of theologians. As part of the presentation, I posed the questions we have been considering. There was active discussion of the questions "What is a disability" and "Are we all disabled?" However, when I posed the question "What are we afraid of?" I had no takers. No one would risk an answer. Finally, I was bold enough to ask, "How about pain, suffering, and death?" My comment did get the conversation going.

We struggle to make sense of disability. The suffering we see scares us. The fear of becoming disabled makes us uncomfortable. People with disabilities assault our cultural norms. We search for security in our values of attractiveness, independence, self-sufficiency, and productivity. "Those people" who can't walk, can't talk, can't hear, can't see, can't learn, and can't take care of themselves violate our comfortable norms and threaten our tentative peace. We are startled by the thought that

God might not care if we are attractive, independent, and productive. And so we keep our distance. We look the other way. We do cursory acts of kindness to stave off guilt. Charles Gourney speaks of "the experience of 'feeling good' after having helped someone with a disability."[18] He goes on to say that "sometimes even 'good' feelings can mask a hidden sense of superiority, a perception that the other is 'different.' "[19]

We cling to the cultural norms of attractiveness, independence, self-sufficiency, and productivity to avoid coming face to face with two of our great fears: we are not perfect and we are not in control. Disability brings the eschatological horizon into sharp focus.

THREE

~

The Experience of People
with Disabilities

*[N]early two-thirds of disabled people had not been to a movie
theatre in the previous year, compared to just 22 percent of the
general population. Seventeen percent of disabled people had not
eaten a meal in a restaurant, although only 5 percent of nondisabled people had avoided dining out. As compared to only 2 percent of all others, 13 percent of disabled people have never shopped
in a grocery store. When pollsters from Louis Harris and Associ-
ates asked disabled people why they remained so separate, 59 percent explained they were afraid to go out. They were afraid of
being mistreated.*[20]

Disability's Dangerous Memory

On July 26, 1990, President George Bush signed the Americans
with Disabilities Act. This landmark civil rights legislation
"provides a clear and comprehensive national mandate for the
elimination of discrimination against individuals with disabilities."[21] This law ushered in a new era for people with disabili-

ties. Notwithstanding the significant strides in this decade, historically, people with disabilities have been, and still are, oppressed.

The term "dangerous memory" is borrowed from the liberation theologian Johannes Metz who uses it to refer to the remembrance of the oppression of the past that acts as a catalyst for the claiming of one's own voice and the courage to challenge oppression.[22] It is in the dangerous memories of oppression that a community finds a sense of dignity. The history of people with disabilities is a minefield of dangerous memories: litanies of inhumane treatment, neglect, exclusion, public and private humiliation, ignorance, bigotry, and death that must not be ignored or forgotten.

The first 275,000 people to go to the gas chambers in Nazi Germany were people with disabilities.[23] *Lebensunwertes Leben*, life unworthy of life, was the view that justified and fueled the extermination of people with disabilities. Many Nazi experiments such as the perfecting of death by legal injection and mass carbon monoxide poisoning were practiced on people with disabilities—beginning with children.

The idea of killing people because of a disability is not confined to the Holocaust. The devaluing of a disabled life is repeated again and again throughout history and is still occurring. People with disabilities have often been the targets of involuntary euthanasia movements. Chilling phrases like "lives not worth living" and "useless eaters" in reference to people with disabilities supported the goals of selective breeding in a very active worldwide eugenics movement in the 1920s and 1930s. Starvation of babies born with various types of disabilities was a common practice for many years in the United States. People with disabilities are often given a "priority" in the assisted suicide movement that is currently unfolding in the United States.[24]

Warehousing of people with mental retardation has been common for centuries. I remember going to pick up my little brother at the institution where he lived before we adopted him.

He lived in a building that was euphemistically called a "dorm," a long, barren room with some forty iron beds with graying white sheets, lined up against the wall. The children were not allowed to have stuffed animals because of fear of germs. The toilet stalls had no doors, and the shower was one large room with a drain where everyone showered together, naked, with a hose-like contraption spewing cold water at them. The depressing part of this story is that he was in a relatively nice place compared to many others. In the late sixties, Geraldo Rivera produced a scathing exposé of the Willowbrook Institution in New York where people with developmental disabilities were living in horrifyingly inhumane circumstances: hundreds of people in overcrowded wards, sitting on the floor with glazed stares, lying naked and unkempt in bed in their own urine and feces, or wandering unsupervised. Neglect, abuse, semi-starvation, overmedication, and no health or dental care were an institutional way of life. Unfortunately, places like Willowbrook were not the exception. A photographic account of this living nightmare can been seen in *Christmas in Purgatory*, a grim and horrifying view of life in the back wards of five institutions. The secretly taken photos "eerily echoed the disturbing photos of emaciated and benumbed survivors of Nazi concentration camps."[25] A series of class action lawsuits followed the exposé of these institutions and began the deinstitutionalization movement, moving some quarter of a million people with disabilities from state institutions to group homes located in the community.

In an article entitled "Public Stripping,"[26] Lisa Blumberg describes the humiliating and common experience of "public stripping" that many disabled people, and especially children, have been routinely subjected to during medical examinations. Privacy and respect are not considered necessary because they were disabled. One thirty-year-old woman with spina bifida tells of her twice yearly childhood examinations where she was examined in a large hospital room, with twenty or more doctors, residents, and physical therapists looking on and discussing her as if she were not even present. Often these examinations were videotaped. She was permitted to wear only her underpants. When she reached puberty, her request to keep her training bra on was flatly denied and was removed by a noticeably irritated doctor. Other people tell similar stories of "public stripping" resulting in life-long trauma and nightmares from this disrespectful and dehumanizing practice.

In his article "The Room of Pain and Loneliness," Edward L. Hooper writes of the rampant abuse of people with disabilities at the hands of their attendants and families. "And abuse is 'out of the closet,' right? We read all the time about abuse: child abuse, spouse abuse, abuse of the elderly. But disability's abuse closet seems as tightly locked as ever teeming with what by all sketchy accounts is a Pandora's box of unspeakable nightmares nobody seems to want to touch."[27] He goes on to tell the story of Tom Zablesky, a man for whom the "closet" was no metaphor. When he was five years old, he fell out of bed at the D.T. Watson Home for Crippled Children and broke his hip. His parents were not told of the injury, and if he cried from the pain, his bed would be moved into a closet where the door would be closed and he would be left for hours, or days on end, until he could "behave." This went on for years. He did not tell his mother about "the closet" until he was thirty-four years old. He thought it was just something he had to endure. There are many reasons why disabled people do not turn in their abusers: fear of things only getting worse, an internalizing of the abuse in thinking somehow they deserve it, or a terrible sense of shame. "People with disabilities endure slaps, punches, burns, isolation, neglect, insults, intimidation, theft, lack of personal care, physical restraints, sexual molestation and more."[28] Hooper claims "we acknowledge spouse abuse, child abuse, elder abuse. But we don't acknowledge disability abuse."[29]

Abuse, neglect, freak shows, public stripping, forced sterilization, extermination—the list of the dark history of the treatment of people with disabilities goes on. I would venture to say that every disabled person has dangerous memories—stories of being humiliated, excluded, and patronized—stories that spawn a group consciousness and a collective memory. A man is asked to go sit in the "Cry Room" at his church because his wheelchair "ruined the decor." A group of children with mental retardation were denied admission to the zoo because they might frighten the monkeys. A man with outstanding academic credentials and excellent field placements tells of going on seventy-five unsuccessful job interviews. A woman with cerebral palsy is asked to leave a restaurant because her presence makes the other patrons "uncomfortable." Until very recently it was not the back of the bus for people who used wheelchairs, it was no bus at all. My purpose in mentioning some of disability's dangerous memories and citing these few examples is not to evoke pity for people with disabilities, but rather to point out that all these memories have one thing in common: they play out society's deep prejudice against people with disabilities.

The Oppression of People with Disabilities

People with disabilities are so oppressed that often others do not even consider them to be oppressed. I once explained how people with disabilities are oppressed to a theologian who teaches liberation theology. After a lengthy explanation on my part, he began to nod and said, "I see your point. . . . Yes, it makes sense. I just never thought of it before." This is a common reaction from nondisabled people—they have just never thought of it. Our language reflects this lack of awareness. There is no vocabulary to describe "disability oppression." There are no words comparable to *homophobia*, or *racism*, or *sexism*, although disability advocates have tried to bring the word *ableism* into usage. Often other uses for the words *disability* and *disabled* are pejorative. For example, a "disabled vehicle" is a nuisance, an eyesore, a problem to be dealt with, and when call waiting is "disabled" it no longer works. R. C. Smith makes the point that "I have seen still more evidence that the prejudice against individuals with disabilities is the most pernicious one held in this country. Unkind words against homosexuals, African-Americans, Hispanics and other minorities at least prompt rebuke from people who, though not members of the group, still recognize the prejudice."[30] Not so for people with disabilities. No one thinks to challenge pejorative remarks about people with disabilities such as describing a clumsy person as a "spaz" or someone who has done something stupid or foolish as a "retard." Nondisabled people think they are complimenting a disabled person when they say, "I don't even think of you as disabled." However, substitute the word *disabled* with the word *black* or *Latin* or *woman* and the hidden bias becomes clear.

What is oppression? In *Interdependence: The Route to Community*, Al Condeluci says, "A person is oppressed when they are held back, either physically or psychologically, from the goals they aspire to, and the norms of society. . . . Oppression is closely linked to devaluation and loss of power."[31] He goes on to say, "The manifestations of oppression have taken hold of our culture and institutions. Oppression against people with disabilities is so intense, that our system has adjusted to it."[32] Much of the time, we are not even aware that entire groups of people are being oppressed. Oppression occurs at both the institutional and cultural levels. On the institutional level, oppression is encountered in housing, employment, education, religion, health services, legal services, transportation, recreation, and within the media. On the cultural level, oppression is encountered in language, standards of behavior, logic systems, within the arts and societal expressions, and particularly in the development and expression of values and norms.[33]

Stereotyping of minority groups is common, and is particularly pervasive with regard to people with disabilities. It is so prevalent that when the disability rights lobbyists in Washington set out to pass the Americans with Disabilities Act (ADA), they made a highly unorthodox strategy decision. There would be little attempt to explain the sweeping antidiscrimination legislation to the press. As the lead ADA lobbyist, Patrisha Wright, of the Disability Rights Education and Defense Fund, put it: "We would have been forced to spend half our time trying to teach reporters what's wrong with their stereotypes of people with disabilities."[34]

Perceptions and stereotyping of people with disabilities are mechanisms that nondisabled people use to figure out and understand the person who is different. Even people who are serious about acting justly often participate in stereotyping, without malice, but without reflection. Stereotyping is inherently dangerous for several reasons. First, these perceptions create invisible but very real barriers that imply a different strand of humanity: keeping the person with a disability at arm's length, viewing the person as "the other." Wolf Wolfensberger, in his classic work *The Principle of Normalization in Human Services*, describes another danger when he says, "When a person is perceived as deviant, he is cast into a role that carries with it powerful expectancies. Strangely enough, these expectancies not only take hold of the mind of the perceiver, but of the perceived person as well."[35] It is well known that people tend to become what they are told they are. Finally, these perceptions and stereotypes are almost always a reflection of the times. There is enormous power in the roles that these perceptions create because legislation, human service principles, medical treatment, personal interactions, theologies, and even fiction tend to reflect these perceptions. It is not a coincidence that shortly after the passage of the ADA, the movie *Forrest Gump*, the unlikely story of a likable young man with multiple disabilities, won numerous Academy Awards and captured the hearts of audiences.

Oppression has devastating and debilitating effects. When people with disabilities openly share their thoughts and feelings, we become aware of how deeply these stereotypes and misperceptions affect their lives.

Oppression causes isolation and a sense of despair. Charles Gourney, in an article entitled "Faith, Despair and Disability," says, "Having a disability can be socially isolating, creating a sense of rejection and fears of abandonment, even by God. The social consequences of physical disability can leave one with a sense that one's life has lost its meaning."[36]

Many people speak of the shame they feel for being disabled. Mary Stainton tells of her experience while hearing Judy Heumann, a disability advocate who is paralyzed and uses a wheelchair, speak about the rights of people with disabilities. Stainton says, "As she spoke, a realization struck me with high voltage intensity and held me; established itself somewhere deep inside of me. 'My God,' I thought, 'I don't have to be ashamed of having a disability.' At some level that was the first time this idea had occurred to me. . . . You don't have to be ashamed of having a disability. You don't have to walk to have worth."[37] She was thirty-two years old at the time and had spent her entire life ashamed of not being able to walk.

According to Gourney, "[p]roblems associated with having a disability go beyond the physical limitations imposed by the disability itself. The sense of exclusion we are likely to experience produces spiritual wounds: anger, low self-esteem, a sense of inferiority, a sense of meaninglessness, despair, even loss of faith."[38] Others describe public humiliation, overwhelming feelings of powerlessness and resentment, or a deep fear of being rejected and dependent.

There is much self-hate associated with disability. Deborah Creamer explains that "People with disabilities have a variety of perspectives about their bodies and embodiment in general. For many of us, the awareness of embodiment is a fact of life—we are always aware of our bodies because of chronic pain, muscle weakness, or limited abilities."[39] Creamer goes on to say, "Society does not value our bodies, which makes it difficult for us to value ourselves. We constantly hear that we are faulty, malformed, broken and sick. Many people with disabilities respond in kind, hating their bodies and their disabilities, wishing they were different."

Oppression creates many practical problems. Marta Russell argues that disabled people are at the very bottom of the socioeconomic ladder[40] and statistical data confirms this thesis. Sixty-eight percent of people with disabilities aged sixteen to sixty-four are not employed.[41] Many people who are working are underemployed. They are more likely to be poor and dependent on public assistance. Forty percent of adults with disabilities live in households with annual earnings of $15,000 or less.[42] Accessible housing is scarce and attendants for people requiring assistance with personal needs are even less available. Social and recreation opportunities are often limited for people with disabilities. Their opportunities for intimacy and interpersonal relationships are limited, and sexuality and sexual needs are often dismissed or ignored. For many people with disabilities, particularly people with developmental disabilities, the only significant relationships they have are with paid staff members. It is not uncommon for people with disabilities to have no friends.

Disability has become somewhat "politically correct" but fictional characters with disabilities of the past were either pathetic or scary, the likes of Captain Hook, Tiny Tim, the Hunchback of Notre Dame, or Long John Silver. My sister pointed out that playing a disabled person is an almost surefire way to capture an Academy Award nomination: Tom Hanks in *Forrest Gump*, Dustin Hoffman in *Rain Man*, Patty Duke in *The Miracle Worker*, Robert DeNiro in *Awakenings*, Daniel Day Lewis in *My Left Foot*, Cliff Robertson in *Charlie*, John Hurt in *Elephant Man*, Jon Voight in *Coming Home*, Tom Cruise in *Born on the Fourth of July*, to name just a few. I am sure there is more to this than just fine acting. Perhaps it reveals society's view of the disabled person as radically other. We believe that an actor who can play someone so different is worthy of special recognition.

Perceptions and Stereotypes about People with Disabilities

There are three overarching patterns of thought and behavior that oppress people with disabilities. These patterns are: domination by nondisabled people, use of oppressive language, and an attitude of low expectations. Perceptions and stereotypes are organized by the categories of historic, religious, and contemporary.

Oppression through Domination by Nondisabled People

People with disabilities are often dominated by nondisabled people. Often this domination is unintentional, or well intended. It is sometimes subtle; sometimes an attempt to assist or to "fix" things and create the outcome the nondisabled person thinks is best for the disabled person. (It is interesting to note that the outcome is often not what the nondisabled person would select for himself or herself.) Often dedicated professionals and concerned family members are involved in this process. It usually involves making major and minor life decisions for the person, often without even asking for input or preference. Consider the ramifications of this type of oppression. How would you like it if you had not been able to decide where or with whom you wanted to live, what type of employment you wanted, or what you wanted to do for leisure activities? Domination sends the strong message that the person is not capable. Huge service systems have developed that are entirely dominated by nondisabled people. People with disabilities must insist on inclusion on governing boards, as staff members in disability organizations, and as spokespeople for the disability movement.

"Disconfirmation"[43] is a term used by disability advocates to describe what happens when nondisabled people pretend that people with disabilities do not exist or that they are incapable of thinking, speaking, deciding, and acting for themselves. I was once eating dinner in a very nice restaurant in Washington, D.C., with a well-known disability activist. He has a law degree, heads a large disability agency, is married with three children, and uses a wheelchair. The waiter looked directly at me and asked, "What will he have?"

Oppression through Language

The words we use to describe people come with an implicit and explicit message. Language can be a way to exclude people, hurt people, and oppress people. People with disabilities have been called derogatory and pejorative terms like "idiots," "retards," "deaf and dumb," "lame," and "spaz." They are referred to by trite or euphemistic terms such as "differently-abled," "physically challenged," "mentally different," and "partially sighted." Discussion about disability is sensationalized and dramatized by terms like "afflicted," "crippled," "victim," and "deformed." "The" is often placed in front of a category such as "the retarded" or "the disabled," effectively creating distance and implying "the other," with no emphasis on the individual person. Sensitivity in language is an important step in the liberating process. A description of appropriate disability language can be found in part III of this book. Anyone who is serious about the inclusion of people with disabilities needs to become familiar with acceptable disability language and use it.

Oppression through an Attitude of Low Expectations

One of my friends has a son with multiple disabilities that include a speech impediment and severe learning disabilities. She rigorously prepared him for his Bar Mitzvah, just as she had done with her three older children. His Bar Mitzvah was a great day for him and for his family. The rabbi adapted the ceremony to fit his needs and the young man did a fine job of reading from the Torah. We were stunned by the number of people who asked her how she could "put him through" the preparation and the ceremony. It was hard work for him, surely frustrating at times, but it was also the grandest of accomplishments, his

Bar Mitzvah, one of the most important events in Jewish life. These comments reveal the pervasive assumption that expectations should be lower for people with disabilities. We almost automatically assume that a disabled person cannot do as much as a nondisabled person and we are almost always surprised when they can. This is why we see so many "heartwarming" stories about the ordinary accomplishments and activities of a person with a disability, and this is why those stories so infuriate disability advocates.

Historic Perceptions

These perceptions provide a look at how people with disabilities have been viewed throughout history. While many of these perceptions are no longer prevalent, vestiges of even the most unenlightened views still remain.

- The person is viewed as a *subhuman organism*.[44] This was a prevalent perception in the nineteenth century and even into the early twentieth century. The pejorative term "vegetable" developed as a result of this perception. In the late 1800s, huge numbers of people with disabilities were put in warehouses with no heating, as it was thought they had no feeling.
- The person is viewed as a *menace to society*,[45] dangerous and likely to do harm to others. Unfortunately, this perception still exists today. Examples of this can be seen at zoning hearings when people with disabilities are moving into a neighborhood.
- The person is seen as an *object of pity*,[46] in need of charity. This is still a common perception as evidenced from telethons, "Jerry's Kids," and poster children. This perception particularly angers disability advocates for it is patronizing and demeaning. Although often well intended, this perception creates an extreme sense of otherness.
- The person is seen as *sick*[47] and their disability is viewed as

an illness. Diagnosis, treatment, and cure are emphasized. It is from this perception that the "medical model" of service developed. This model has been pervasive and widespread, focusing on diagnosis, treatment, and cure. While some people become disabled as a result of illness, most people with disabilities are not sick; an illness is a separate and not necessarily related experience.

- The person is viewed as a *burden to society*, making no contribution and draining off scarce resources. Current proposed federal policy as well as the concept of managed care support this perception.
- The person becomes an *object of ridicule*[48] and is made the butt of jokes or encouraged to act in inappropriate ways which others find amusing. Often the person is so happy to be receiving attention that he or she is a willing participant.
- The person is viewed as an *eternal child*.[49] This creates a situation where reasonable developmental demands are not made and the individuals are not held accountable for their actions. This perception also promotes treating a person as if they were a child in an adult body, which denies the person's sexuality and can lead to inappropriate behavior. Adults with disabilities often speak of being "infantilized," spoken to and treated like babies or children.
- The person is viewed as *bizarre and grotesque* and is seen as a freak; sometimes an interesting novelty or a frightening sight. Displays of persons with disabilities as sideshows in carnivals used to be common practice. Examples of this can still be found in Ripley's Believe It or Not museums.

Religious Perceptions

Some of these perceptions are drawn from interpretations of stories about disability in the Hebrew and Christian scriptures. Others are a result of interpretations of theological concepts.

- The person is thought to be *possessed by demons*. It is likely that the people described as "possessed" had epilepsy or another type of seizure disorder.

- The person is seen as *lacking adequate faith*, suggesting if they had more faith, they would be cured. Many people with disabilities tell stories of how strangers approach them suggesting that if they had more faith they would be able to stand up and walk.
- The person is viewed as a *holy innocent*, without sin, incapable of any wrongdoing, saved by virtue of their disability.[50] Often people with mental retardation are told they don't need the sacraments because they are already going to heaven.
- In spite of the fact that Jesus makes it clear that disability is not *caused by sin*,[51] there are many people who view having a disability or giving birth to a child with a disability as a punishment for sin. This creates extremely painful, sometimes lifelong feelings of guilt and shame.[52]
- The person is viewed as a *prophet*, one sent with a special message communicated by or through their disability. All people are potential message bearers for God, not just people whom we perceive as different.

Perhaps the most harmful religious perception that plagues people with disabilities is the idea that they are automatically "the least of my people"[53] because of their disability. It is true that many people with disabilities are poor and oppressed and, in fact, are the people Jesus is referring to in his mandate for social justice in Matthew's Gospel. However, we must remember that their poverty and oppression are a result of the way they are perceived and treated by society. They are not necessarily "the least" because they happen to have a disability.

Contemporary Perceptions

As the disability community develops an identity as a group with minority status, new perceptions and stereotypes are emerging.

- If successful and accomplished, the person is seen as a *"supercrip."* This creates false expectations for all people with disabilities. As within the general population, there are a small percentage of people with disabilities who are overachievers.
- The person is seen as *special*. Actually a reversal of the sub-human perception, the person is seen as so different they must have a distinct designation.
- The person is *devalued*, seen as without ability and capabilities. This is evidenced by the fact that so many people with disabilities are unemployed or underemployed.
- The person is viewed as *broken* and in need of fixing. This is often referred to as the mechanical model.
- The person is treated as if they are *invisible*, as if they are not present, as if they do not exist. People share stories of being spoken about as if they were not present, or having questions directed to someone else as if they were not there.
- The experience of being disabled is *romanticized*, seen as having special status or an aura of mystery. This is a reflection of the political correctness now associated with disability issues.

How Should People with Disabilities Be Perceived?

This discussion begs the obvious question: How should people with disabilities be perceived? There is more than one answer to this question. First, people with disabilities, like all of us, should be perceived as unique individuals, created in the image and likeness of God, with great gifts and talents to share, and as people who are inherently valuable and of inestimable worth. Pope John Paul II, in his "Address to the International Conference on the Concerns of Persons with Disabilities," said, "Every human person is the subject of fundamental rights which are inalienable, inviolable and indivisible. Every human being, is always worthy of maximum respect and has the right to express his or her dignity as a person fully."[54] All of us are entitled to live with dignity and respect.

The second point is perhaps not so obvious. People with disabilities need to be perceived as people with disabilities. The correct and fine principles of dignity and respect must not be construed or interpreted as reducing everyone to sameness, by erasing, if you will, the reality of a person's disability or suggesting that, within the designs of dignity and respect, disability can be forgotten or appropriated. When nondisabled people exhibit unwillingness to reflect critically upon and respond to the self-articulated experiences of people with disabilities, or attempt to ignore, reduce, or erase another person's experience of embodiment, this becomes yet another form of oppression.

FOUR

~

An Historical Overview of the Disability Movement

The history of the disability movement is rooted in its radical pluralism. Stephen Hawking, an internationally known physicist, who is paralyzed and sometimes referred to as the most brilliant man in the world, and James, a friend of mine with profound mental retardation and severe physical disabilities, who is dependent on public assistance, have equal standing in the disability movement.[55] Hence, the paradox and strength of the movement. Within the disability movement there are many parallel movements: people with developmental disabilities, people with physical disabilities, people who are deaf, people with autism, and people with head trauma injuries, to name just a few. Each group has different agendas, issues, and life situations that relate directly to particular types of disability. Their struggles are quite different and very much the same. Their activities and interests overlap and intertwine, and their influences upon each other have been significant. Each group would narrate the history of the disability movement differently through their particular lens. I have made every effort to do justice to the diversity of the movement in this brief overview of the history of the disability movement; however, the reader is asked to remember that this sketch is far from comprehensive. My purpose is limited to giving the reader a general sense of the historical activity of the disability movement through a description of some of the key people, events, and legislation that have shaped disability history. I hope to show how, over the span of about thirty years, people with all types of disabilities and their families and friends forged a dynamic alliance that culminated in the Rose Garden of the White House with the signing of the Americans with Disabilities Act on July 26, 1990. This historic event was the beginning of a new era for people with disabilities that continues to develop and extend in many different ways.

Early History

Historians of disability date the beginning of the contemporary disability movement to the early 1960s when people with disabilities entered history with greater visibility and a new vision for their lives. Prior to that time, beginning over a century ago, there was scattered disability activity. In 1850, deaf people established local organizations to advocate for their interests. During the Depression, the League of the Physically Handicapped staged sit-ins at federal offices to protest antidisability discrimination by the government. In the mid 1940s, after World War II, the Paralyzed Veterans of America was founded. During the 1950s, parents of children with disabilities began to organize into self-help groups. In the 1960s, people with disabilities and their families, along with professionals, began to demand a place for people with disabilities in the mainstream of American life. It was through this type of activity that disability became a civil rights issue setting the stage for the birth of the disability rights movement.

Rosemary Kennedy and Ed Roberts

At the risk of oversimplification, the beginnings of the modern disability movement can be traced to two people: Ed Roberts, a man with severe physical disabilities who lived on the West Coast, and Rosemary Kennedy, a woman with mental retardation who lived on the East Coast and whose brother happened to be the President of the United States. During the same approximate time period, a series of events was occurring in Berkeley, California, and in Washington, D.C., that would establish a new course, a new visibility, and a new vision for people with disabilities.

Born in 1918, in the midst of the worldwide flu epidemic, Rosemary Kennedy, who had mild mental retardation, was the fourth child born to Joseph and Rose Kennedy. When she was in her early twenties, her father made the decision to allow a prefrontal lobotomy to be performed on Rosemary in hopes that it would help her occasional violent outbursts. This was not an uncommon solution at the time to a condition that has since been known to respond well to medication and behavior management programs. The surgery was unsuccessful, dramatically changing Rosemary's ability to function, and she was subsequently institutionalized in 1941. When questioned, the family told inquiring reporters that she was in a convent. In the spring of 1962, Eunice Kennedy Shriver, with the blessing of her father and her brother, President Kennedy, wrote an article for the *Saturday Evening Post* telling the truth about Rosemary. *U.S. News and World Report* calls this article and the events that followed "one of the biggest moments and perhaps the most important contribution the Kennedys made to the nation."[56] To a generation accustomed to seeing people with mental retardation at school, at the mall, working at Wendy's, and starring on *L.A. Law*, the decision of the Kennedy family to disclose the fact that Rosemary was mentally retarded does not seem particularly noteworthy. However, Rosemary's "coming out" was indeed an extraordinary event. Prior to that time, having a child with mental retardation was a secret shrouded in shame. If a child was kept at home, it is likely that guests were not invited to the home, and it was not unusual for a disabled child never to leave the house, even to go outside and play. I once gave a woman a tour of a facility where I worked who told me that her mentally retarded brother, who was ambulatory, had excellent speech, and could dress and feed himself, had not been out of the house in forty years! Often a child would be institutionalized from birth. Sometimes other children in the family were not even told they had a sibling. Public education was not available to children with mental retardation; the idea of a job or social life was unheard of; and inhumane warehousing was common practice. When I ponder this terrible waste of lives, I am filled with sadness. The Kennedy family's disclosure lifted the veil of secrecy surrounding mental retardation, and began a new era of visibility for people with disabilities.

At the same time, across the country, in California, Ed Roberts was wheeling into class at the University of California at Berkeley. His journey into that classroom had been a long haul, and there were many who thought Ed Roberts should be locked up and forgotten just as Rosemary Kennedy had been. Ed and his family, however, had other ideas. Roberts, who died in 1995, was the greatest of visionaries: tenacious, brilliant, with a keen political sense and a wonderful wit. When he was fourteen, he contracted polio and within twenty-four hours was paralyzed and in an iron lung. The early years were most difficult.

> I decided I wanted to die. I was fourteen years old. Now, it's very hard to kill yourself in a hospital with everything set up to save your life. But the mind is a powerful thing. I stopped eating. They started to force feed me. It was really demeaning. I dropped to 54 pounds. My last special duty nurse left, and the next day I decide I wanted to live. You see, that was the big turning point. Up until then, these nurses were available and doing things for me around the clock. I didn't have to make decisions for myself because they were always there. When they finally left, that is

when I realized that I could have life, despite what everyone was saying. I could make choices and that is freedom. I started to eat again.[57]

Ed recounts that he heard his mother ask the doctor whether he would live or die. Answering in front of him, the doctor told his mother: "It would be best if he were to die because if he lives he'll be a vegetable for the rest of his life." Ed's response to the doctor's proclamation always makes me smile. "So I decided to be an artichoke—a little prickly on the outside but with a big heart on the inside. You know, the vegetables of the world are uniting, and we are not going away."[58]

Ed went to school for three years by telephone from his home. Finally, before his senior year, he faced his fear of being seen by people. He describes his first day of school. "I arrived at lunch time. Everyone turned to look at me. I looked at someone, right in the eyes, and they turned and looked away. That was me. I looked at someone, right in the eyes, and they turned and looked away. That was when I realized that maybe it wasn't my problem. I checked myself out and realized two things. First, their looking at me didn't hurt physically, and second, I realized, hey, it's like being a star—and I've been a star ever since."[59]

The first of many political battles began when Ed was told he could not graduate from high school because he had not taken physical education and driver's education. When he and his family protested the decision, the vice-principal admonished him. "Now Eddie, you wouldn't want a cheap diploma, would you?" His mother took it to the school board who sided with Ed, and awarded him his well-earned high school diploma. After a few years at a local community college, Ed applied to the University of California at Berkeley. He was flatly denied admission. "We tried cripples and they don't work" was the reason given. Adamant about attending Berkeley to study political science, he sued the university and won. The same semester that James Meredith was escorted into an all-white classroom

Ed rolled into a Berkeley classroom. The headlines of the local newspapers reported the event: "Helpless Cripple Attends U.C. Classes." Because there were no accessible dorms, Ed lived in a ward in Cowell Hospital, on the edge of campus. Within a few years, there were twelve other men who were wheelchair users living there. The "rolling quads," as they called themselves, soon became a familiar sight around the university and the group developed a strength from each other that led to a sense of exhilarating empowerment. Ed was in the right place at the right time for during the 1960s Berkeley was a hotbed of student movements and social change.

As he realized that disability issues were civil rights issues, Ed began to study civil rights movements. He read Saul Alinsky's *Rules for Radicals,* and tells how the leadership of the feminist movement would allow him to attend their meetings. Listening intently, he began to see a connection between experiences. He met with Stokeley Carmichael and others in the Black Power movement to "tell them we were all fighting the same civil rights battle." He began to organize and participate in demonstrations and to encourage other people with disabilities to "get out there and get arrested . . . not just for anything, but for the cause. Getting arrested for what you believe in can really change your perspective, it can strengthen your resolve."[60]

With funding from a federal grant, Ed along with several other disabled students, founded the Physically Disabled Students Program (PDSP) at Berkeley. The program had three main components: a pool of attendants and emergency attendants, a group of engineers who would repair wheelchairs, and, in time, an accessible housing list. The PDSP was unique because it was conceived, organized, and run by people with disabilities. These were radical and new ideas because people like Ed Roberts were not thought to be capable of managing their own lives.

Ed finished all the course work for a Ph.D. at Berkeley and taught in an inner-city school for several years while continuing to work on disability issues. He was responsible for founding the Centers for Independent Living (CIL) that revolutionized how people with disabilities live by giving them control over their own lives. In 1975, Governor Jerry Brown named Roberts to be the director of the state's Department of Vocational Rehabilitation. There was great irony to this, as this same bureau once told him that he would never be employable. He later became the President of the World Council on Disability. Ed Roberts died in 1995 at the age of 56. I had the privilege of coordinating one of his memorial services where great stories about his life were shared. Often called the "father of the disability movement," his legacy and spirit live on in the disability community.

There are countless other people such as Justin Dart, Judith Heumann, Wade Blank, Frank Bowe, Robert Burgdorf, Jr., Mary Jane Owen, Patrisha Wright, Robert Perske, and Wolf Wolfsenberger, among others, whose vision has shaped and continues to inspire the disability movement.

Major Events and Legislation of the Disability Movement[61]

A few of the major events and legislative victories of the disability movement are described here to give the reader some sense of the progression of activity that has occurred over the past thirty years. This list is not comprehensive and only highlights significant milestones, as well as describes some of the state and public laws that are disability related. Many of these laws build on each other; in other words, the law has been expanded and revised over time.

1961
President's Council for Mental Retardation

At the urging of his sister, Eunice Kennedy Shriver, President John F. Kennedy made disability issues a priority and developed the President's Panel on Mental Retardation. The panel, comprised of professionals and parents, undertook a survey of existing programs and treatments and presented a comprehensive report, entitled *A Proposed Program for National Action to Combat Mental Retardation*. Organized under eight broad headings, there were 112 recommendations including the development of a national plan for community-based care, improved educational opportunities, more comprehensive social services, and a reduction of the number of people living in large, congregate care facilities. President Kennedy made the implementation of this report a priority, and there was great expansion in research, programs, and visibility. This activity laid the foundation for the normalization and deinstitutionalization movements that would follow in the coming years. It was significant in that the panel was among the first of many governmental committees that would influence disability policy on the federal level.

1962
President's Council on Employment

The President's Committee on the Employment of the Physically Handicapped is renamed the President's Committee on the Employment of the Handicapped, reflecting its increased interest in employment issues affecting people with a wider range of disabilities, including cognitive disabilities and mental illness.

1964
Civil Rights Act of 1964

This Civil Rights Act outlaws discrimination on the basis of race in public accommodations and employment as well as in federally assisted programs. It becomes a model for subsequent disability rights legislation.

1965

Social Security Act Amendment (P.L. 89–97)

In 1965, an amendment to the Social Security Act establishes Medicare and Medicaid. Individuals who are permanently and totally disabled, including about fifteen percent of whom are persons with mental retardation, are Medicaid eligible.

1972

Supplemental Security Income Act (SSI)

This amendment to the Social Security Act creates supplemental income and relieves families of the financial responsibility of caring for their adult disabled children. It consolidates existing federal programs for people who are disabled but not eligible for Social Security Disability Insurance.

1972

PARC v. The State of Pennsylvania
Mills v. Board of Education

These two lawsuits issue rulings that disabled children cannot be excluded from public schools. These decisions will be cited by advocates during the public hearings leading to the passage of the Education for All Handicapped Children Act of 1975.

1972

Incorporation of the First Center
of Independent Living

The first Center for Independent Living, founded by Ed Roberts, attempts to replicate the vision of the Physically Disabled Students Program at Berkeley. Even the title was revolutionary. Most people had never thought of independence as a possibility for people with disabilities; however, Roberts was clear about his goals and what he wanted. The Center for Independent Living was organized to provide the vision and resources needed to get people out into the community. Not a social service agency, CILs are also models for advocacy-based organizations, for as Roberts put it, "no longer would we tolerate being spoken for."[62] The by-laws mandate that at least fifty-one percent of the staff and board must be people with disabilities. Today there are some 370 CILs all around the country which have assisted over 140,000 people.

1972
Lawsuit Filed for the Closing of the Willowbrook
Institution; New York Association for Retarded
Citizens v. Carey

After visiting the Willowbrook Institution, Senator Robert Kennedy said that it was "less comfortable and cheerful than the cages in which we put our animals in the zoo." The name "Willowbrook" became synonymous with neglect and abuse and the horrors of institutionalization. Following a grand jury investigation after a ten-year-old boy was scalded to death by faulty plumbing, and a twelve-year-old boy was strangled while in restraints, the parents of the residents filed suit to end the appalling conditions at that institution. There have been many other class action lawsuits filed on behalf of people with disabilities living in institutions that have resulted in moving thousands of people into community-based living arrangements.

1973
Rehabilitation Act of 1973 (P.L. 930–112, Section 504)

The passage of the act, especially Section 504, is a major milestone in the disability rights movement for it openly confronts discrimination against people with disabilities. Section 504 specifically prohibits programs receiving federal funds from discriminating against "otherwise qualified handicapped individuals." This act increases the amount of funding authorized under the Rehabilitation Act of 1921 to over one billion dollars for the training and placement of people with mental and physical handicaps into employment. This act makes explicit congressional intent that vocational rehabilitation services be made available to people with severe disabilities. This law gives disability advocates greater power in demanding access for people with disabilities. The concepts and language that came from the lawsuits filed relating to this act, such as "reasonable accommodation" and "undue burden," form the basis for the Americans with Disabilities Act of 1990.

1974
Founding of People First

People First, the largest U.S. organization composed of and led by people with developmental and cognitive disabilities, is founded in Salem, Oregon. The primary purpose of the organization is self-advocacy, and members of this organization effectively participate in a variety of political and legal disability rights activities including a successful class action lawsuit in Tennessee. Currently, there are sixty chapters throughout the United States, and thirty throughout the world.

1975
Education for All Handicapped Children
(P. L. 94–142)

Public Law 94–142 changed life for children with disabilities and their families in a dramatic and permanent way. For the first time, public education becomes available to children with any type of disability, and this law mandates a free and appropriate public education in the least restrictive environment. Individual Education Programs (IEPs) are mandated with special education and related services designed to meet the unique, individual needs of each child. This law was modified in 1986 to extend protection to disabled children ages three to five. This act is the one of the cornerstones of disability legislation. Since its passage, millions of disabled children have been educated, radically changing the experience of being disabled.

The politics and philosophy of the disability movement is played out in a very particular way in the arena of education. An entire discipline of "special educators" has emerged: administrators and teachers who develop, supervise, and teach children with disabilities. Incorporating these students into the public education system has been costly and complicated. One of the most important educational issues centers around the controversial and hotly debated question of what is called "mainstreaming": the practice of having disabled students and nondisabled students sharing the same facilities and classrooms, whenever possible. The opposite of mainstreaming, segregation of disabled students, is unacceptable to many parents and disability advocates.

1976

A disability rights organization, Disabled in Action, pickets the United Cerebral Palsy Telethon in New York City calling telethons "demeaning and paternalistic shows which celebrate and encourage pity."

Passage of an amendment to the Higher Education Act of 1972 offers services to college students with physical disabilities.

1977
Protest over Section 504 of the Rehabilitation Act

This protest is a watershed event in the disability rights movement. Activists staged demonstrations in ten cities and occupied the federal offices of Health, Education and Welfare (HEW) to force the Carter Administration to issue regulations implementing Section 504 of the Rehab Act of 1973. The occupation in San Francisco lasted nearly a month and was a great source of empowerment for people with disabilities. The stories of this protest are legendary within the disability movement, and I recommend reading accounts of the sit-in as a way to gain insight into the movement. On April 28, HEW Secretary Joseph Califano signed the regulations.

1979
Founding of the Disability Rights Education and Defense Fund (DREDF)

Founded in Berkeley, California, this organization is the nation's preeminent disability rights legal advocacy center and was a key player in the landmark litigation and lobbying in the 1980s and 1990s, including the passage of the Americans with Disabilities Act.

1981
Katie Beckett Amendment

The story of this amendment to Medicaid funding options is a favorite of mine. Katie Beckett was a three-year-old girl who lived in Iowa. She had multiple disabilities, used a ventilator, and required a variety of services. The state offered her mother a residential placement at the cost of $12,000 a month. Mrs. Beckett wanted to keep Katie at home and care for her but she needed help to do so. The cost of keeping Katie at home was $4,000 a month, but the state would not pay, even though there was a huge cost saving as well as the great benefit of Katie being with her family. Mrs. Beckett wrote a letter that somehow made its way to President Ronald Reagan. President Reagan agreed with Mrs. Beckett's logic and took the idea to Congress resulting in the amendment of Medicaid requirements to allow funding for families who wished to keep their children at home. Katie, now twenty-three, still lives at home. Just recently, a woman in Rhode Island told me how she is able to keep her daughter at home with her because of funding from the Katie Beckett amendment.

1982
The Telecommunications for the Disabled Act of 1982

This Act requires that the Federal Communications Commission (FCC) establish regulations to ensure reasonable access to the telephone network for people who are deaf, hard of hearing, or speech impaired. It requires that certain telephones considered essential be hearing-aid compatible. Essential phones were defined by Congress as pay phones, emergency phones, and telephones often used by people who were deaf or hard of hearing.

1988
Gallaudet University Protest

The protest at Gallaudet University, the world's only liberal arts university for deaf students is a watershed event for the disabilities rights movement. On March 6 and 7, 1988, students shut down their campus, declaring that it would remain closed until Gallaudet's board of trustees reversed its decision of the previous day to appoint Elisabeth Ann Zinser, a hearing person, as president. The students issued four non-negotiable demands: (1) Zinser's resignation and the appointment of a deaf president; (2) the resignation of the chairman of the Board of Trustees; (3) an increase in the deaf representation on the board to fifty-one percent; and (4) no reprisals against the protesters. The trustees rejected all the demands and the students prepared for an indefinite strike. Strong support from the alumni and the faculty added momentum to the students' strike forcing Zinser to resign and the trustees to agree to the demands of the students, appointing Irving King Jordan, dean of the College of Arts and Science as the president. The "Deaf President Now," as this protest is known, drew national and international attention to some of the central issues of the disability rights movement demonstrating the power of united political action.

1990
The Passage of the Americans with Disabilities Act

The intent of the Americans with Disabilities Act is to ensure that people with disabilities receive equal opportunity to participate in society free from discrimination. The law challenges the stereotypes and perceptions that have kept people with disabilities oppressed, dependent, and unable to realize their potential. The law mandates equal access for people with disabilities to employment, state and local government services, transportation, public accommodations and services provided by private entities, and telecommunications.

The law is divided into five sections:

Title I:	Employment
Title II:	Public Services
	Subtitle A: State and Local Governments
	Subtitle B: Public Transportation
Title III:	Public Accommodations
Title IV:	Telecommunications
Title V:	Miscellaneous Provisions

Title I prohibits businesses with fifteen or more employees from discriminating against qualified individuals with disabilities. Employees must provide "reasonable accommodations" for people with disabilities who are otherwise qualified to do the job as long as the accommodation does not pose an "undue hardship" on the employer. A religious organization or entity may give preference in the hiring process to individuals of a particular religion to perform work connected with the carrying on of its activities. Those involved in religious ministry, such as ministers, priests, or rabbis, are not covered by Title I.

Title II prohibits discrimination in public services provided by state and local governments and by the National Railroad Passenger Corporation. The law mandates that all government facilities and services must be accessible. Title II prohibits discrimination in public mass transportation.

Title III prohibits discrimination against people with disabilities in public accommodations, such as restaurants, hotels, theaters, retail stores, health clubs, museums, libraries, parks, private schools, and day care centers. Private clubs and religious organizations are exempt.

Title IV addresses communication and mandates that "communication carriers"—telephone and telecommunication companies—make services available. These services include telecommunications devices for the deaf, or TDD (commonly called TTY), as well as relay services for individuals who do not have TTY. Title IV also requires federally funded television programming to be closed caption.

Title V contains various miscellaneous provisions including exemptions to insurance providers, and stipulates that nothing in the ADA should be seen as negating or limiting previous disability laws.

The impact of the ADA has been widespread, giving people with disabilities greater access to ordinary life. It has made the political agenda of the disability community a part of the national political agenda and given people with disabilities visibility and recourse. Conversely, it has brought some disappointment, as it has not created an overnight change in the way people with disabilities are treated by society.

The exemption of religious organizations is particularly troubling, especially because of the forceful lobbying that occurred to ensure exemption by some, but not all, religious communities. Arguments for exemptions ranged from the need for separation of church and state to the claim that it is what religious organizations should be doing without legal prodding. Certainly, lobbying for this exemption has contributed to the tension between the disability rights movement and the religious community. It is hopeful to note that many religious organizations have followed the trends and are making efforts to provide accommodations to people with disabilities.

1990–2000
Post ADA

The passage of the ADA has by no means been the end of the disability rights movement. In many ways, it has been the beginning of a new era of visibility and access for people with disabilities. Georgia voters elected an openly disabled candidate, Max Cleland, to the U.S. Senate. Senator Bob Dole, a person with a visible disability, ran for President without trying to hide the extent of his disability as Franklin Roosevelt did earlier in the century. Disability advocates insisted that President Roosevelt's disability be acknowledged in the Roosevelt Memorial in Washington, D.C. Jerry's Orphans, a group of disabled people who find the telethons demeaning, staged its first annual picket of the Jerry Lewis Muscular Dystrophy Association telethon, protesting the demeaning way people with disabilities are portrayed in the telethon. Robert Williams became the Commissioner of the Administration on Developmental Disabilities, the first disabled person to hold the post. In 1996, Sandra Jensen became the first person with Down syndrome to receive a heart-lung transplant. Originally denied this surgery, disability advocates lobbied the Stanford University medical staff and reversed their decisions. ADA lawsuits, on the state, federal, and Supreme Court levels, began to interpret the law giving both victories and setbacks to the disability movement. The assisted suicide movement and the concept of rationing of health care, both of which target people with disabilities, became areas of advocacy for disability rights advocates. The disability rights movement continued to expand in many directions as people with disabilities chart their own courses and futures.

~

The Philosophical Concepts of the Disability Movement

While the reader probably has some sense of contemporary disability philosophy by this point, the purpose of this section is to reiterate systematically the philosophical concepts that drive the disability movement and to describe the rise of a disability culture. This is perhaps the most important section of this book for unless nondisabled people change the way they think about disability, disabled people will always be oppressed. When I lecture on disability, people often want me to skip over the philosophy and tell them what they should do. I tell them the first thing they should "do" is pay attention to disability philosophy for only if they think differently will they act differently.

People with disabilities desire independence and equality, and are demanding full inclusion in all aspects of life. The philosophical concepts of the disability movement support, reflect, and relate to the desire for independence, equality, and dignity.

Disability has its own language, terminologies, and concepts to describe its philosophical underpinnings. Understanding the meaning and intent of this language provides a direct view into the thinking of the disability movement. The selection I present is representative and inclusive so therefore not every concept I mention applies to every disabled person or subgroup. Some of these concepts, as indicated, are particular to specific groups within the movement. The reader should be aware that other disability activists might present these philosophical concepts differently or perhaps even disagree with my selections; however, on the whole, I believe this presents a balanced description.

"Consumer" Control

Simply stated, this means that people with disabilities want to be in charge of their own lives. The word *consumer* is sometimes used because traditionally speaking those who purchase goods and services have power. It is considered preferable to client, patient, or resident. Historically, in rehabilitation settings it was common for medical personnel, social workers, rehab counselors, and family members to decide what was "best" for the disabled person, either without consulting them or ignoring their wishes. Available choices were few and supported the stereotype that people with disabilities are less capable and need protection. People with disabilities began to view themselves as consumers of the services that were being provided and demanded to be in charge of making their own decisions. Conceived in the Centers for Independent Living movement, consumer control puts the power of decision making in the hands of the disabled person.

Advocacy

Advocacy is a central activity within the disability field. Advocacy, quite simply, means to plead your own cause or the cause of another. What do advocates do? How do they create change? How do they challenge systems and misperceptions? There are many different types of advocacy. One person directly assisting another person in finding a solution for a problem is case advocacy. A group of people challenging an unfair situation is class advocacy. The many lawsuits that resulted in the closing of institutions around the country are an example of legal advocacy. System advocacy is when an individual or organization works to correct an injustice. Helping someone find a job or housing is advocacy. Speaking up when someone uses a derogatory term like "retard" is advocacy. Working to improve accessibility in the places you frequent is advocacy. Self-advocacy is when the person with the disability advocates for their own interests. This is the best form of advocacy.

Al Condeluci names four vital elements to advocacy: passion, position, presence, and perseverance. He believes passion is the starting point for advocacy. He calls position the stand we take on the injustice that arouses our passion. He sees presence as forging appropriate strategies to advance our position and creating a viable presence. He defines perseverance as accepting the facts that fighting oppression is difficult work, real change is slow to occur, and a long-term commitment is required. He encourages advocates to find ways to include others, renew themselves, and celebrate together.[63]

The "Principle of Normalization" and "Social Role Valorization"

The principle of normalization and social role valorization are highly developed social theories that have been enormously influential in shaping positive approaches in the developmental disabilities field and beyond. In 1972, Wolf Wolfensberger published a book entitled *The Principle of Normalization in Human Services*, which developed a concept borrowed from Scandinavia. The philosophy espoused by Wolfensberger in this book revolutionized the ways services were provided to people with mental retardation. "Normalization" became "a captivating catchword standing for a whole new ideology of human management." The principle of normalization is based on the idea that people with mental retardation should have the same patterns and conditions of everyday life as mainstream society. The concept of normalization is deceptively simple; however, it has far-reaching implications that impact every area of life and demands a rethinking of everything from living arrangements to education to appearance. It recognizes the role of ideology, culture-specific normativity, and the power of perceptions and is a sociological model as opposed to medical or therapeutic model. The principle of normalization has been critiqued for using the nondisabled person as the normative standard, and the phrase and concept are no longer widely used, although generations of special educators were trained in this concept. Wolfensberger later began to use the concept of "social role valorization" suggesting the idea that when people are placed in roles that are socially valued—such as friend, employee, or consumer of goods and services—they are viewed differently, which changes the quality of their social interactions with others.

Self-Determination

In the last decade, the concept of self-determination has emerged, particularly within the developmental disabilities community. Self-determination is defined as the process whereby an individual is able to control his or her life, achieve self-defined goals, and participate fully in society. The principles that guide this concept are freedom, authority, support, responsibility, and confirmation. Individuals with disabilities seeking to improve their lives use the self-determination model, as do those who seek to assist them (family members, support and service systems, and communities). There are numerous self-determination centers and programs springing up around the country that are interactive collaborative networks working to change the nature of support and services for individuals with disabilities using the principles of self-determination.

Community Inclusion

Sometimes called community integration, community inclusion refers to the experience of being a valued member of the community in which an individual lives, along with having the opportunity to be involved in all aspects of the community, including physical, social, political, educational, and economic integration. Being involved in the community means using services such as shops, hairdressers, doctors, and banking, exercising the right to vote, and enjoying what the community has to offer including leisure and recreation activities such as sporting events, restaurants, parks, and beaches. Involvement in community events and the use of services often provide ways to know others and make friends. Access to community life is something that many people take for granted; however, people with disabilities have often been denied this opportunity because of inaccessibility or institutional living.

The Dignity of Risk

The phrase "the dignity of risk" was developed by Robert Perske and refers to well-meaning attempts to overprotect the disabled person.[64] Perske argues that people with disabilities are often denied their fair share of risk taking. He claims this is sometimes done in clever ways by limiting spheres of behavior and interactions in the community, jobs, recreation, and relationships with the opposite sex. While the intent of these actions are to "protect," "comfort," "keep safe," "take care," "watch," and are usually benevolent and helpful, they tend, if acted on exclusively or excessively, to keep people from experiencing the risk taking or ordinary life which is necessary for normal human growth and development.

Natural Supports

"Natural supports" are the things that help us to be independent and productive; in other words, they support us in our natural settings. Natural supports are always individualized and vary from person to person. The natural supports that I need are not the same as the natural supports that you need. A voice-activated light switch is a natural support and so is a lowered kitchen counter. A wheelchair, a personal attendant, and an adapted van might make one person independent. Another may need transportation to work and a computer station that can be voice operated. All of us use natural supports. They are the equipment and services that assist us in accomplishing our goals. If I didn't have contact lenses and reliable childcare, I could not write this book or teach in a university. Natural supports are particularly significant for people with disabilities for they permit greater independence and freedom.

Supported Employment and Supported Living

The concepts of supported employment and supported living build on the concept of natural supports. Supported employment has been very successful in helping people with disabilities find and keep good jobs. In a supported employment situation, an individual has a job coach who goes with them to work to help them learn to do their job, to help them adjust to the workplace and the workplace adjust to the disabled person, and to make sure that the job tasks are completed in a timely and professional manner while the individual is training.

A supported living situation involves assisting people in ways that enable them to receive the support they need to live in a home that they want. This includes being able to choose where they live, and with whom they live, and how they want to live. It involves providing individualized natural supports. Issues such as ownership and control are primary concerns related to supported living.

Assistive Technology and Adaptive Equipment

Nothing has changed things more for people with disabilities than assistive technology and adaptive equipment. Technology transforms limitations into opportunities. The Technology Related Assistance for Individuals with Disabilities Act of 1988 defines assistive technology as "any item, piece of equipment, or product system that is used to increase, maintain, or improve functional capabilities of individuals with disabilities." Some examples of assistive technology are sip and puff controls for wheelchairs, lifts to transfer physically disabled people from a wheelchair to a shower or automobile, and speech synthesizers. Emerging technology has endless capabilities for enhancing many activities and offers people with disabilities extraordinary possibilities for communication, independence, and integration.

Universal Design

Universal design is based on the concept that environments, buildings, and furnishings should be functional, practical, and simple to use for everyone—disabled and nondisabled people alike. Universal design eliminates unnecessary stairs, places light switches strategically, and designs kitchens and bathrooms to meet a wide variety of needs. A curb cut is helpful to a mother with a stroller, bikers and roller-bladers, an elderly man with a grocery cart, a woman who has just had knee surgery, and a teenager who uses a wheelchair. Door handles that are easy to open and manipulate are good for a person who is carrying a child, a bookbag, or a suitcase, a person with arthritis, or a person with limited upper-body strength or range. Large numerals on clocks, ovens, and signage are great for middle-aged people, for just about anyone in low-light situations, as well as for people with vision impairments. When my children were little I was always grateful when there was room for them in the larger bathroom stalls. A great benefit of universal design is that as a person grows older, they are more likely to be able to remain in a home that has been universally designed.

From Concepts to Culture

The disability movement has given rise to a disability culture. Historian Paul Longmore calls disability culture "the second phase" of the disability rights movement. The first phase, he wrote in *The Disability Rag and Resource*, "has been a quest for civil rights, for equal access and equal opportunity, for inclusion. The second phase is a quest for collective identity. Even as the unfinished work of the first phase continues, the task in the second phase is to explore or create a disability culture."[65] Longmore sees this phase as redefining disability from the inside. In other words, people with disabilities are using their own experiences of disability to create their own culture. Cheryl Marie Wade explains how this is occurring:

> It's finding a history, naming and claiming ancestors, heroes. As "invisibles" our history is hidden from us, our heroes buried in the pages unnamed, unrecognized. Disability culture is about naming, about recognizing. Naming and claiming our heroes. Like Helen Keller. Oh, not the miracle worker version we're all so familiar with, but the social reformer, the activist who tried so desperately to use her celebrity to tell the truth of disability: that it has far more to do with poverty, oppression and the restriction of choices than it has to do with wilted muscles or milky eyes.[66]

Disability literature, poetry, art, films, theatre, social critiques, magazines, and other publications are emerging as disability culture develops.

Many disabled people are claiming that, in and of itself, there is nothing wrong with or abnormal about having a disability. They view their limitations not in terms of their disabilities but more in terms of attitudes and stereotypes and external barriers created by society. People with disabilities are becoming comfortable with who they are and do not necessarily wish to be nondisabled. They claim that a life with disabilities is far from necessarily tragic or pitiable. They point to a list of great disabled figures such as Ludwig van Beethoven, John Milton, Flannery O'Connor, Julius Caesar, and Franklin Delano Roosevelt. Many call this newfound freedom and understanding "disability pride"—which perhaps sounds radical—but so once did

"Black is beautiful" and "gay pride." "Disability pride," writes Laura Hershey, "is a feeling that is not easy to come by in this segregated, inaccessible, often discriminatory world . . . [but] without pride our movement can never develop."[67] Cyndi Jones, editor of disability rights *Mainstream Magazine*, sums it up well. Once during an interview, she was asked, "But what if a miracle cure were developed overnight? Wouldn't you eagerly swallow a magic pill that would wipe away the lingering paralysis of your polio and let you walk again?" She answers quickly "No. It's the same thing as asking a black person would he change the color of his skin."[68]

Conclusion

In this section of the book, I presented statistical and general information about the worldwide disability community and explored the topic of disability as a social and cultural reality. The dark history of the treatment of people with disabilities was presented along with an explanation of the way certain perceptions and stereotypes keep people with disabilities oppressed. An overview of the contemporary disability rights movement from both an historic and philosophical perspective was offered followed by a description of the emerging disability culture. At this point I turn to the second task of this book: an examination of the Christian tradition from a disability perspective and ask two foundational questions. First, how does emerging disability culture challenge and inform the Christian tradition? And, second, why do I propose a theology of access as the meeting place of contemporary disability culture and God, Jesus Christ, the Holy Spirit, and the church?

PART II

REINTERPRETING THE CHRISTIAN TRADITION FROM A DISABILITY PERSPECTIVE

~

SIX

Informing the Tradition: The Need for New Theological Interpretations

Gather us in,
The lost and forsaken,
Gather us in,
The blind and the lame.

From the song "Gather Us In"
by Marty Haugen

I, the Lord of wind and flame,
I will tend the poor and lame,
I will set a feast for them.

From the song "Here I Am, Lord"
Lyrics by Dan Schutte, S.J.

Amazing Grace, how sweet the sound
That saved a wretch like me
I once was lost, but now am found
Was blind, but now I see.

From the Shaker hymn "Amazing Grace"

I am strength for all the despairing,
I am healing for the ones who dwell in shame
All the blind will see, the lame will all run free,
And all will know my name.

From the song, "You Are Mine"
Lyrics by David Haas

People are not given disabilities so that nondisabled Christians can sing about how happy they are that they're not disabled—blind, lame or otherwise.

People do not have disabilities so that Christians can test their faith by trying to heal them—or so nondisabled people can chalk up points with God by being charitable to them.

People have disabilities because people are human, and disability is a natural part of the human state.

Josie Byzek
Ragged Edge, November/December 2000

How Does a Disability Perspective Inform and Challenge the Christian Tradition?

Central to the development of a meaningful and useful theology of access is a careful examination of the Christian tradition that allows a contemporary disability perspective to both challenge and inform the Christian tradition. In this part, I examine the tradition in two ways. First, in this chapter, by a discussion of four key theological notions that I suggest are foundational to disability theology: Christian anthropology, embodiment, spirituality, and social justice.[1] In the next chapter, by an examination of three primary "texts" in the Christian tradition: Scripture, liturgy, and sacraments. It is these "texts" and theological categories that form the foundation of the theology of access I present in part III. This part closes with an explanation of why I propose a theology of access and with a discussion of the challenges and limits of access and inclusion.

An All-Encompassing
Christian Anthropology

Is everyone created in God's image? What is the Christian understanding of human existence? What does it mean to be human in light of the Incarnation? A theology of disability demands an all-encompassing Christian anthropology. The first step is a critique of the ideology of normalcy.

The utter mystery of God is revealed in the variety found in the human person, all of whom are created in God's likeness and image. People with disabilities give us full access to the human condition and demand that we expand our definition of "normal" and stop making the automatic assumption that a person with a disability is "abnormal." Barrett Shaw explains this well:

> Because many kinds of difference are feared and shunned, the disability experience has been a different experience. We are told there are now about 49 million people with disabilities in America—about one in five. There are many kinds of disability and many degrees of each. Some are more stigmatized than others. But the fact that one in five Americans has one ought to make it evident that having a disability is no more abnormal than having straight hair or an epicanthic fold. Variety is normal. Even if perfection were possible, it would be dull.[2]

Very few of us agree with Mr. Shaw. We do not have an inclusive anthropology. We have our own ideas about what is "normal" as well as what is "abnormal." And normal almost never includes a disability. What is normal? The white, heterosexual, nondisabled, tall, slim man? Where does that leave the rest of us, I wonder? A narrow or limited understanding of what is normal oppresses people with disabilities. As long as we think there is something wrong with using a wheelchair to get around, people with disabilities will always be oppressed. We go through the world in many different ways. There is nothing abnormal about not being able to see. There is nothing wrong with not having a high I.Q., anymore than there is something wrong with being a woman or being a homosexual. As long as we have a limited understanding of what is normal, people with disabilities will always be oppressed.

Contemporary culture worships the glamorous and denies an awkward vision of the *imago dei*. Beldon Lane says:

> Our culture substitutes the glamorous for the grotesque, denying this awkward vision of the *imago dei*. . . . If we define a person exclusively in terms of rational ability and productivity, someone with Down syndrome will inevitably appear less than whole. The eccentric, the ugly, the abnormal lie beyond the measure of our societal norms. We are left with a stylized and truncated humanity, dangerously imagining itself complete."[3]

Does this imply that God might not care if we are attractive, independent, and productive? People with disabilities become "the ultimate threat to self-definition."[4]

A specifically Christian anthropology demands that we broaden our narrow understanding of personhood and challenge the cultural norms that stylize and truncate humanity by suggesting all are not created in God's image. For indeed, everyone is created in the image of God.

How is the Incarnation, the saving event of God becoming human and disappearing into humanity, related to disability? In a *Study Guide on Disability* titled "Is Christ Disabled?" produced by the Lutheran Church, the following is said, "The Incarnation involves God becoming human in Jesus of Nazareth. God assumes human form and thereby participates fully in humanness. Humanness means frailty, weaknesses, illnesses, accidents, impairments, aging and many other marks of our mortality."[5] A specifically Christian anthropology demands a rethinking and a reappropriation of frailty, weakness, illness, impairments, and disability. Certainly the crucifixion was disabling. Gaping holes in hands and feet from nail wounds cause disfigurement and limit mobility, and yet the marks of Jesus' own mortality—the scars of the crucifixion—were not erased from the body of the Risen Christ.

An Inclusive Theology of Embodiment

The social location of disability is the body. Nothing is more fundamental to disability theology than an inclusive theology of embodiment. Just as feminist theology must interpret reproduction, disability theology must interpret physicality. Embodiment is a very practical matter for many people with disabilities. Related to embodiment are practical issues such as health, sexuality, medical care, bodily functions, clothing, grooming, and aesthetics and spiritual issues such as prayer, mysticism, sacramental access, and redemption.

Body shame is neither a new thing nor confined only to people with disabilities. We live in a society where almost everyone hates his or her body. We live in a society where teenage girls are paid millions literally to starve themselves to death, and are idolized for doing so. We live in a culture where middle-aged, otherwise intelligent people are plunged into despair as they begin to age. Almost everyone wishes they looked different. An inclusive theology of embodiment stands against these things and stands for acceptance.

Christianity has a long-standing tradition of hierarchical dualism, often suggesting that the "spirit" is preferable to the "flesh." This concept denies our embodiment as a source of God's goodness and revelation. Susan Ross describes another problem dualisms can cause. "Dualisms such as nature/history, body/spirit, female/male are oppositional—one side is seen over and against the other—as well as hierarchical—one side must control the other."[6] Nondisabled over disabled can be added to this list. Ross goes on to claim that "Violence against women, children, nature, that is the animal world and the fragile ecosystem that supports all life on the planet, can result when one side rejects the other as evil."[7] Certainly the oppression and marginalization of people with disabilities have been one result of the dualism of spirit over body, and nondisabled over disabled. Disability theology must stand against the temptation toward disembodiment, and the idea that the spirit is superior to the physical body; instead, it must encourage an integration of the body and spirit.

Barbara Peterson writes convincingly of the need for an inclusive theology of embodiment, calling for "the expansive and diverse vision of redeemed embodiment."[8] She believes that "if we take seriously that God is restoring the goodness of all creation, then we cannot deny that our present bodies, as they are, are participating in this goodness."[9] Our different bodies are "redeemed bodies full of inclusive goodness."[10] Together, these redeemed bodies have the potential to become an inclusive community of faith and hope where no body is marginalized. "Explicitly, redeemed embodiment as inclusion means that we can call good overlooked, denied, and unexpected expressions of embodied life."[11] To do less denies our common humanity, and God's own self-expression and sacramental presence in our lives.

Disability Spirituality:
Things Are Not What They Seem

When I was a young professional, the color of my pantyhose was very important to me. I liked a light beige or off-white color and I made sure I stayed away from the tan shades. As ridiculous as this sounds, it is true. I used to spend lots of time assessing my pantyhose and the pantyhose of others. An experience early in my career in disability changed my perspective on this strange fixation.

In 1977, I left my wonderful job as assistant to the headmistress at Carrollton School of the Sacred Heart. Five minutes from my home, I was able to bring my baby boy, Chris, to work with me. I was surrounded by bright, talented, and happy young girls. I enjoyed a special relationship with the Religious of the Sacred Heart to whom I owe my spiritual formation. When I was offered a job in a fledgling disability agency, fraught with financial, political, and management problems, I knew I had to go. The facility was far from my home and the salary was lower. There were no beautiful young women with bright futures; instead, there were one hundred and twenty children with profound and severe mental retardation and no futures. Reluctantly, I told my boss and good friend, Sister Ann Taylor, RSCJ, that I was leaving Carrollton. I remember sobbing as I drove out of the school on my last day of work and wondering where all this was taking me.

Even with my exposure to disability through my brother, I was still not prepared for what I encountered in my new job. The people served by the agency where I worked are those who are usually hidden from view. They are what some in our society would call "vegetables." Collectively, they had every type of physical and developmental disability imaginable. Most of the people were unable to speak, many were unable to walk, and many required assistance with even the most basic life skills— dressing, toileting, eating—a dependency that would make most of us recoil in horror. In spite of these extraordinary frailties (or perhaps because of them), a deep sense of peace and kindness permeated this unusual place.

I was very happy at my new job. I loved my colleagues and the work was very challenging. I considered myself a busy person with many important things to do. One morning, during my first year on the job, when I was getting ready for a business trip to Tallahassee, I had an experience that changed me forever. I remember I was wearing a pretty red suit and sheer light beige pantyhose. I left my office and went to visit one of my favorites, Jason, a fourteen-year-old boy. Jason was very small for his age, with an oversized head. His hair grew in patches because of the many shunts that had been put in his brain. His arms were twisted, and because of a bone disease his legs were often broken. On this day, both legs were in casts. Jason could not speak or feed himself and had to be bathed and diapered with special care because of his brittle bones. I know Jason lived in constant pain as he would often moan softly. Although Jason was blind and could not speak, he always recognized my voice and would begin clapping when he heard me call his name. I came upon him and one of our staff members, a humble and lovely person named Felicia Santos. Felicia was quite a woman. She was truly compassionate, hardworking, dedicated to her work and the children, and so happy. She was also a great advocate! She often knew what was wrong with the children before the doctors could diagnosis a problem. I remember once she challenged a doctor when a little boy named Jimmy wasn't feeling well. She told the doctor Jimmy had an earache. The doctor said Jimmy did not have an earache. Felicia was furious and went to a supervisor, who deferred to the doctor. When Jimmy, who could not speak, came down with a high fever and a terrible ear infection within twenty-four hours, the doctor apologized to Felicia. Shortly after that, the doctor began to ask for diagnostic advice. Jason and Felicia were devoted to each other. When I came upon them, Felicia was leaning forward, talking softly to Jason. He was smiling. I stood for a few minutes before speaking and watched their interaction. What I witnessed between them was the purest of love—the kind of love that asks for nothing in return. The only thing I could think of was the words from Mark's Gospel account of the Transfiguration: "and looking around, they saw only Jesus." For that is what I saw. Standing there in my designer suit, with the right color pantyhose, and my list of "important things to do" still on my desk, I was rooted to the floor. I realized that things are not what they seem. I realized that Jason had more to give me than I had to give him. I knew that in her simplicity and humility, Felicia knew more about life than I did. I understood that within the brokenness, wholeness, and hiddenness of Jason and within the kindness, patience, and generosity of Felicia, God was being revealed. I knew what I saw was very pleasing to God and that the angels would someday lead Jason and Felicia into Paradise. I left work that day changed forever. Twenty-four years have passed since that revelation-filled morning. It still amazes me that God would reveal Godself so clearly to a girl concerned with such silly things as the color of her pantyhose.

A meditation on disability takes us right to the heart of the mystery of God's love and self-communication. Disability raises haunting spiritual questions. One senses that within the mystery of disability, valuable insight and knowledge can be found. How does one access this insight? Why are people disabled? What does disability tell us about God? How do we make sense of the suffering associated with disability? Disability is a dramatic reminder that God's ways are not our ways. God is not what we expect. How do we attempt to understand a God who creates precious babies born with no arms and legs or with severe mental retardation? How do we make sense of a God of power and might whose sons and daughters have accidents that leave them quadriplegics or deeply fatigued from life-altering chronic illness? And what about God the Creator who allows His only Son to be severely mutilated just before he dies alone on the cross? Clearly, these are not our ways. For if we are honest, who among us wants to be the parents of the child born with no arms or legs? Who among us wants to become a person with a disability on our way home from work tonight? Who among us wants to be dependent on others? Who among us wants to be crucified?

Avoidance of pain and suffering is a lifelong pursuit for all of us. Even Jesus wanted to avoid pain and suffering. Even those who don't pray echo Jesus in asking God "to let this cup pass me by." And, yet, no matter how we may try, at sometime in our life the dreaded cup overflowing with suffering is passed to us.

Throughout the ages, theologians have struggled to understand and communicate the mystery of suffering. Disability often brings a very visible kind of suffering. Physical pain and weakness, exclusion from the mainstream of society, significantly increased family responsibilities, blatant discrimination, and economic injustice are examples of some of the common experiences that cause suffering within the lives of people with disabilities.

I am skeptical of the idea that we learn something special from the suffering of people with disabilities, or the suffering of anyone, for that matter. I do not believe that some people are disabled to teach people who are not disabled important lessons. I am more comfortable with the somewhat out-of-date and old-fashioned notion that there is a spirituality of brokenness through which God communicates with all of us. Suffering is suffering. And it definitely comes with message. It is perhaps what Beldon Lane speaks of when he describes what "used to be called the *via negativa*—the discovery of God's presence in brokenness, weakness, renunciation and despair."[12]

We struggle to make sense of disability. The suffering we see scares us. The fear of becoming disabled, of pain and of death, makes us uncomfortable. A meditation on disability forces us to examine our own lives for clues suggesting God's presence where we least expect it. We bump right into the great paradoxes of the Christian message. The sacramentality of the world is revealed. What is obscure and in some ways beyond our understanding is that we encounter great beauty in what is thought to be, at first, ugly; we experience transformation through suffering; and we realize wholeness through recognizing our poverty and not our capacity. We encounter God's grace and mystery in the places we least expect or want to find them. We have to acknowledge "that grace rarely comes in the shape of a gentle invitation to change. More often than not it appears in some form of an assault—something we are first tempted to flee."[13] We come to realize that God's grace is not what we thought it would be, and that things are not what they seem.

A Call to Justice: Is There a Need for a Critical Liberation Theology of Disability?

The experiences of being disabled must be considered from a social justice perspective because people with disabilities have been, and still are, oppressed and marginalized. A report issued by the United Nations contends that worldwide conditions for people with disabilities are worsening: "Handicapped people remain outcasts around the world, living in shame and squalor among populations lacking not only in resources to help them but also in understanding. And with the numbers growing rapidly, their plight is getting worse . . . we have a catastrophic human rights situation . . . they [disabled persons] are a group without power."[14] In *Nothing About Us Without Us*, James I. Charlton says that "the vast majority of people with disabilities have always been poor, powerless, and degraded."[15] He calls for an analysis, which considers how the overarching structures of society create this oppression.

I have known, first hand, of this oppression, since I was a teenager. In 1965, when I was fifteen years old, I went on a car trip with my best friend, Patti, and her mother, Mary Ragan. We drove from Miami to Leesburg, Florida, to take a look at the orange groves that Mrs. Ragan had recently purchased. I remember being excited about the trip. We set off early one morning in the Ragans' light blue DeSoto. Patti was driving, Mrs. Ragan was in the front seat, and I was in the back. Mrs. Ragan's bulky metal wheelchair was in the trunk, along with our luggage and the wooden board that she used to slide in and out of the car into her chair.

During a visit to Miami to see her parents when Patti was a little girl, Mrs. Ragan had contracted polio. She was in an iron lung for several years. During that time, her husband divorced her and she and Patti moved from California and settled in Miami. Paralyzed except for the use of two fingers on her right hand, Mrs. Ragan supported herself and Patti by doing tax work and bookkeeping. She had an entrepreneurial spirit that resulted in several business ventures, including the orange groves we were going to visit and an ice cream parlor and candy store named "Patti's Candies" that was always filled with teenagers. Mrs. Ragan was a very peppy and popular person. She had an indomitable spirit, possessed a profound wisdom and a wry and playful sense of humor. Adults and teenagers alike were very attracted to her and loved to be around her. After my parents, who were wise enough to encourage my relationship with her, Mrs. Ragan was the most influential person in my life during my formative teen years.

Our trip to Leesburg took about five hours. We chatted the whole way and Mrs. Ragan let Patti and me pick the radio station. I remember that I was happy that "I Wanna Hold Your Hand" by the Beatles came on the radio three times. We arrived in the area in the mid-afternoon and went to check into the motel where we had reservations for our three-night stay. The man behind the desk glanced at Mrs. Ragan in her wheelchair and her two teenage sidekicks. He pointed his chin at the wheelchair and flatly informed us, "that thing won't fit through the door." With a dignity that no teenager could ever comprehend, Mrs. Ragan guided us out of the motel and back to the car where her daughter helped to slide her back into the car. She waited in the car during our next two tries that yielded the same results. Finally, as it was growing dark, we found a little motel where the owner kindly offered to take off both the outside door and the bathroom door so Mrs. Ragan's chair could fit. We spent three nights there—all together in one room—with both our bathroom and hall door wide open to the world. I am glad that I was too young to realize just how vulnerable we were.

This experience has stayed with me. Although I was your basic, self-centered, clueless teenager, even I knew that something terribly wrong had happened. I can still see Mrs. Ragan sitting in the front seat with her head lowered as we searched for a place to stay. I remember being sick to my stomach and thinking I was carsick. Years later, when I learned the language of liberation and the concepts of social justice, I realized that I was not carsick. That queasy feeling in my stomach was from the anxiety produced by witnessing the humiliation of exclusion, oppression, and injustice for the first time.

Liberation theologies make the claims that oppression is due to profound social injustice, and that oppression is contrary to the central message of the gospel which proclaims that all people are called to live with joy, hope, and grace in God's love. The narrative of the dangerous memories of people with disabilities in part I makes clear the pervasive and widespread oppression of people with disabilities. When Gustavo Gutiérrez describes the "irruption of the poor," he is speaking of those who until now were "absent" from history and are gradually becoming "present" in it.[16] This is an apt way to describe people with disabilities: absent from history and gradually becoming a part of it. As they have gradually become a part of history, their oppression has been revealed. The Christian community must respond to this oppression. One of the ways this response might occur is in the form of a critical liberation theology of disability.

Latin American liberation theology. North American Feminist liberation theology. Gay liberation theology. Black liberation theology. Hispanic/Latino liberation theology. African liberation theology. Asian liberation theology. Ecotheology of liberation. *Mujerista* liberation theology. The list of different voices speaking of oppression, poverty, and injustice has been echoing around the world since the 1960s when theologians in Latin America dared to relate the widespread poverty and suffering of their people to social and political structures. Prior to this time, there was no such thing as "liberation" theology. The normative theological conversation was developed and controlled primarily by European men in university settings with a discourse that had a philosophical and theoretical bent. Liberation theologies, on the other hand, are set against the eschatological backdrop of the promises of the Kingdom and, by deliberate design, are experience based and practical in nature.

They are built around an acknowledgment of the suffering of real people who, because of oppressive structures, find themselves in situations of marginalization and poverty. One of the primary purposes of liberation theologies is systematically to challenge the dominant political, economic, and cultural structures in which a group of persons, be it women, homosexuals, Hispanics, or people with disabilities, are subordinated and excluded from full participation in the life of the society.

Paul J. Wojda describes the primary themes of liberation theology as: (1) a preferential option for the poor which demands "solidarity with the victims of unjust oppression in the form of a concrete commitment to or actual involvement in their emancipator struggles for justice"; (2) a unity of theory and practice that demands not only seeing the reality of oppression but responding to this reality with action resulting in an "intersection of theory and praxis"; (3) an ideological critique that unmasks the false ideologies that conceal oppressive economic and social structures and creates alternative ideologies that envision a social order free of inequality; (4) a use of Scripture that interprets the biblical drama of creation and redemption as disclosing a God who, in the people of Israel and the person of Jesus Christ, liberates and takes the side of the poor and vulnerable.[17]

Liberation theologies are generally developed in two steps:[18] The first step is a description of the human situation being addressed and the unmasking of political ideologies and structures that are oppressive. This step makes use of the social sciences, history, and political theory, acknowledging that the social sciences have mediated a social anthropology and a theory of knowledge that interface with the theological imagination. Step two presents theological teaching in response to the human dilemma described in step one. This is done by interpreting Christian doctrines referring to human existence in social terms, by maintaining that the "option for the poor" should be the foundation and intentional basis of the whole church, and by stressing participation in social action for the liberation of the poor and oppressed.

Sometimes called theology from "the underside" or "from below," liberation theologies can be subversive. They have the potential to redistribute power, to call commonly accepted practices into question, to give a voice to the voiceless, and to upset the *status quo*. With these kinds of challenges, liberation theologies often make the powerful and privileged uncomfortable. The Roman Catholic Church, as a significantly powerful and privileged institution, has validly criticized liberation theology for its political constructs, its dependence on Marxist or socialist ideologies, and its focus on the institutional dimensions of sin as opposed to individual sin. Perhaps, too, it does not care for a critique that names the hierarchical church as the privileged class. Nonetheless, Pope John Paul II has affirmed the "useful and necessary" character of liberation theologies.[19]

Liberation theologies are bold enough to ask, "What are we doing wrong?" and "How can things be righted?" Liberation theologies are grounded in the experience and perspective of the oppressed. The ways in which oppression has occurred and the ways in which it can be counteracted make up the particulars of a specific liberation theology. To that end, first and foremost, people with disabilities must tell their own stories, recover their own histories, and claim their own voice and language. These stories must guide the development of a liberation theology of disability. The very particular oppression and struggles of disabled people must be named and articulated in order for an authentic theology to be constructed.

The components of a critical liberation theology of disability would include many of the topics in this book from a somewhat different perspective. There are perhaps other areas that would need to be considered as different voices and perspectives emerge. These might include the politics and economics of disability, or disability theologies specific to the feminist or African-American experience, which would extend and nuance the content of the theological reflection.

What are the advantages and disadvantages of creating a disability liberation theology? What do liberation theologies do?

They offer a sense of identity to the members of a formerly un-recognized group. They encourage conversation and dialogue. They help groups develop their narratives and claim their histories. They explain the particular oppression of a group to interested others. They unmask ideologies and structures that are oppressive. But do they foster social change and, equally importantly, do they foster access and inclusion? Are the people in Latin America, where liberation theology was born, any better off than they were before liberation theology? Do liberation theologies ever reach the people who need to hear them? Do they impact or change oppressive structures?

There are at least three reasons why I think that a disability liberation theology would be helpful. First, liberation theologies have an "edge" to them—the collective voice can be loud and a little grating. Sometimes the people speaking are actually and rightly angry. They resist patronization, which I believe would be helpful to people with disabilities, for domination and patronization by nondisabled people are two of the critical problems people with disabilities encounter. Second, liberation theologies tend to have a set of central claims about a particular group and their experiences. I think these claims would be very helpful as disability theologies begin to emerge. In the introduction, I articulated what I believe some central claims about disability should be, beginning with the idea that people with disabilities share fully in human nature and are not in any way inferior to people who are not disabled. Claims such as these would be useful in developing sound Christological, ecclesiological, pneumatological, and sacramental theologies in relationship to disability, which would eventually impact pastoral practice. Even if others disagreed with the claims, it would be a starting point for conversation. Finally, liberation theologies are the place where oppressed groups currently locate themselves within the theological field and inclusion might be of value in that it would create a known identity.

When considering the disadvantages of a liberation theology of disability, several points come to mind. Is the very nature of liberation theology "exclusionary"? One of the strengths of the disability movement is that many people in the movement are nondisabled. Contemporary disability philosophy is built on the idea of integration and inclusion. If the first and primary goal of any disability theology is access and inclusion, could a disability liberation theology ultimately work against inclusion by further segregating the group? Once you are identified with a group, is that where you are likely to remain? Do segregated groups have more or less opportunity for conversation?

After presenting some highlights of my research and material to a group of graduate theology students, I posed the question of whether we need a disability liberation theology. The consensus was yes, they felt that my work had been consciousness raising for them. There was agreement that the oppression of people with disabilities needs to be made known, and that a liberation theology might be a good way to give voice to this oppression. I remain uncertain, perhaps believing that the impetus for a theology of this nature needs to come from the disability community.

Conclusion

In this chapter, I addressed the topics of Christian anthropology, embodiment, social justice, and spirituality from a disability perspective with the intent of suggesting new interpretations for these theological categories. These interpretations reflect the principles that guide my work, particularly the ideas that people with disabilities share fully in human nature, that a meditation on disability is a meditation on the mystery of God's love and the great paradoxes of Christianity, that people with disabilities are oppressed, and that the Christian community must acknowledge and respond to this oppression.

New theological interpretations, however, are not enough. I believe a critique of the tradition is also necessary. In Tracy's critical correlation, the major expressions of the Christian tradition that he calls "texts" must be interpreted, in this case, from a disability perspective. As a starting point, three primary Christian "texts" will be considered: Scripture, liturgy, and sacraments.

~

SEVEN

Challenging the Tradition: A Critique of Three Primary "Texts"

Scriptural Exegesis

Theological reflection on disability begins with scriptural exegesis because Scripture is the normative expression of divine revelation within the Christian tradition. There are some twenty-six Scripture passages and stories about people with disabilities in the Gospels. It would be naive to think that stories from the most read book in the history of the world do not have great influence. I argue that the way the disability passages are often interpreted contributes to the oppression and marginalization of people with disabilities. Therefore, scriptural exegesis of the disability passages begins with a "hermeneutic of suspicion," asking a question not unlike the question posed by many feminist theologians when they inquire if Scripture, with its decidedly patriarchal bias, can be relevant and meaningful to women.[20] Likewise, disability advocates must ask difficult questions such as: Do the Scriptures have an "ableist" bias that ultimately oppresses people with disabilities?[21] Does the focus on "curing and healing" in the disability Scripture stories encourage the thinking that there is something inherently wrong with being disabled? Does the notion that there is connection between sin, illness, and disability and the concept that there is something fundamentally wrong with being disabled contribute to the marginalization of people with disabilities? Are there ways to interpret these passages that are empowering to people with disabilities?

The Problem of the Disability Narratives in the Gospels[22]

Generally speaking, most interpretations of the disability narratives in the four Gospels are a problem for people with disabilities.[23] Some people with disabilities go so far as to call the disability Scriptures "texts of terror." At the very least, some interpretations of these passages are problematic for several reasons. First, they create a "fix-it" mentality suggesting the idea that getting rid of a disability is the ideal. Second, they often perpetrate marginalization by portraying people with disabilities as marginalized figures. Finally, within the Christian tradition an unfortunate and harmful "cult of healing" has developed that misinterprets the relationship between faith and healing.

Colleen Grant, in her article "Reinterpreting the Healing Narratives," makes the point that some healing stories

> present problems for people with disabilities who seek acceptance and full participation in the life and liturgy of the Church. Although the primary aim of these narratives is to convey the Christological claim of Jesus' divine authority on earth, they have also served as proof of the moral imperfection of people with illness or disability.[24]

Disabled people are often marginalized figures in the Gospels. This marginalization is seen in the following ways. With the exception of Bartimaeus, the other disabled people in the

Gospels are nameless, and to be nameless in the ancient world showed a complete lack of social status. Most disabled people in the Gospels are poor, unemployed, beggars, or servants. This continues today as people with disabilities in the United States are three times more likely to live below the poverty level.[25] In some Gospel stories, people with disabilities are patronized, treated with contempt, publicly rebuked and humiliated, screamed at, and spoken at, instead of spoken to. And often, when Jesus notices the disabled person, he is treated differently and better.[26]

It is possible to interpret the disability passages in a way that is empowering to people with disabilities. To do so, requires a rethinking of the content and context of the disability passages. It requires "a new way of thinking," as they say in the disability rights movement.[27] The following seven points are the basis of interpreting these passages in a new way.

1. recognizing the difference between illness and disability
2. recognizing the difference between healing and curing
3. separating of the disability and illness passages based on these distinctions
4. analyzing the disability passages to describe the scope of Jesus' ministry to people with disabilities
5. critiquing the "healing cult" in the Christian tradition
6. explaining why Jesus took away the disabilities of some people
7. describing the disabilities of the human Jesus and the Risen Christ

Separating the Disability/Illness Passages

The passages where Jesus cures someone who is ill versus takes away a disability must be separated because having an illness and having a disability is not the same thing. In total, there are approximately seventy-five passages where Jesus cures an illness, raises a person from the dead, or takes away a disability.

Of these seventy-five, approximately twenty-six are disability related. Being sick and being disabled are not the same thing, although as I mentioned earlier, people with disabilities are sometimes subject to a "medical model" which attempts to treat their disability as an illness that can be cured. It is true that in some instances an illness will cause a disability to occur, just as an accident or the aging process can cause a disability to occur; however, illness and disability are not the same thing, and people with disabilities are not sick. A person who uses a wheelchair who has the flu is sick. When she recovers from the flu, she is no longer sick.

The Difference between Curing and Healing

Although they are often used interchangeably, there is a nuanced and significant difference between "healing" and "curing." The word *cure* is defined as: "restoration of health, recovery from disease; a method or course of medical treatment used to restore health,"[28] while the definition for *heal* has a much different focus: "to restore to health or soundness; to set right; **or to restore a person to spiritual wholeness.**"[29] Cures, in the sense of recovery from disease, or restoration of physical health, do occur occasionally, but are not ordinary events, nor the central message of the gospel, nor the point of our faith in Jesus Christ. A central message of the gospel, however, is that we can be restored to spiritual wholeness. Much of Jesus' active ministry on earth was aimed at the restoration of spiritual wholeness, which he offered to the entire community, not just to those who were sick or disabled. He was healing, then, many more people than he was curing. Our own hearts and spirits can be healed, again and again, in Christ, by the power of the Holy Spirit, often through the experience of the sacramental life of the Christian community. It is this type of healing that should be an ordinary event in the Christian life, and is a perfect example of Karl Rahner's notion of the mysticism of everyday ordinary life.

Analysis of the Disability Passages

There are a total of twenty-two narratives where Jesus removes a disability from a person. In many cases, these narratives are a retelling of the same event. While there are a few passages that refer to groups of people being cured,[30] the number of individuals that Jesus cures is only somewhere between thirteen and fourteen, depending on how the retelling of the same story is assigned. The chart on the following page describes the people who were healed by Jesus and the location of the story within each Gospel. I have attempted, when possible, to describe the nature of their disabilities in contemporary terms and have not used the often pejorative term commonly used in the Scriptures and commentaries to describe the disability. I have also noted the method that Jesus used to remove the disability.

Of the fourteen people Jesus healed, only one person has a name (Bartimaeus). There is only one woman, the woman with curvature of the spine. Only one person does not ask for healing, the man who was born blind. Several of the passages are related to the faith of the individual, or used for the purpose of Christological identification. In numerous passages, Jesus steps outside of the law or norms of his times, to assist a person with a disability.

Sometimes people with disabilities feel as though they are objectified in the disability Scripture passages, as if the only purpose they serve is to be healed. Although the cultural context in which the authors of the Gospels wrote does sometimes make it appear this is the case, I do not believe that the actions of Jesus himself indicate that he has objectified people with disabilities. To the contrary, he treated each person as an individual, paying attention to their unique situation by using a variety of methods to remove their disabilities.

What Was Jesus Up To?

Jesus was drawn to people who were marginalized by society; hence, it would make sense that he would be attracted to people

An Overview of the Disability Passages in the Four Gospels

Passage	Matt (8)	Mark (6)	Luke (6)	John (2)
1. Man who was paralyzed on mat *Method: Verbal*	9: 1–8 (no hole in the roof)	2: 1–12 (hole in the roof)	5: 17–26 (hole in the roof)	
2. Man who was paralyzed for 38 years *Method: Verbal*				5: 1–9
3. Servant who was paralyzed[31] *Method: Verbal, from another location*	8: 5–13			
4. Man with the "withered" hand *Method: Asked man to stretch out his hand*	12: 9–14	3: 1–6	6: 6–11	
5. Two men who were blind *Method: Touched eyes*	9: 27–31 20: 29–34			
6. Bartimaeus[32] *Method: Verbal*		10: 46–52	18: 35–43 (unnamed)	
7. Man who could not speak and was "possessed" *Method: Verbal*	9: 32–34		11: 14–15	
8. Man who was blind and could not speak *Method: Unknown*	12: 22–23			
9. Man who was blind with a speech impediment *Method: Took him aside, put fingers in his ears, spat and touched his tongue, and prayed*		7: 31–37		
10. Boy with epilepsy *Method: Verbal*	17: 14–21	9: 14–29	9: 37–43	
11. Woman with curvature of the spine *Method: Laid his hands on her*			13: 10–17	
12. Man who was born blind *Method: Made mud and spread it on his eyes*				9: 1–41
13. Blind man at Bethsaida *Method: Took man by the hand, went outside the village, put saliva on his eyes and laid his hands on his eyes, repeated*		8: 22–26		

with disabilities who were extremely marginalized in the ancient world. From an historic standpoint, disability had a cruel social construct in first-century Jerusalem. As Josie Byzek points out, "There was no Americans with Disabilities Act. Only one occupation was open to a person who could not walk or who was blind: begging. There were no wheelchairs. If an ancient Israelite could not walk, he crawled, or stayed indoors until he died. It was a miserable existence."[33] The description of people with disabilities languishing in the five porticos at the pool in Bethsaida offers a vivid picture of this miserable existence.[34] Jesus' interest in including people with disabilities in his ministry is consistent with his mission to preach the good news of inclusion in the divine salvific plan.

The thirtysome years that Jesus walked the earth was the most extraordinary time in the history of the world. God, in the flesh, became a person and entered into the human condition. Extraordinary things happened that were never meant to become ordinary events. Why did Jesus cure people? Raise people from the dead? Take away their disabilities? He did these things so people would believe he was God. Human nature being what it is, they would never have believed him otherwise. The Gospel writers make numerous references to the response of the people to Jesus' miracles. "We've never seen anything like this!" they exclaim in Mark's Gospel.[35] In Matthew's Gospel, the people "were astounded beyond measure"[36] "and proclaimed, "Never before has anything like this been seen in Israel."[37] Jesus needed at least some people to believe that he was God so he could fulfill his salvific mission.

The story of the four men who carried their friend who was paralyzed to see Jesus illustrates this point well. "When Jesus saw their faith, he said to the paralyzed man, "Take heart, son; your sins are forgiven."[38] Josie Byzek points out that he forgave the man in his paralyzed state.[39] Jesus goes on in the passage to clarify his purpose. "For which do you think is easier to say, 'Your sins are forgiven,' or to say, 'Stand up and walk'? But so that you may know that the Son of Man has authority to forgive sins." He then said to the paralyzed man, "stand up, take your bed and go to your home." He took the man's disability away to prove to the people that he was God. He did not need to take his disability away to forgive his sins. The forgiving of the man's sins were far more important than the removal of his disability. The reality that our sins are forgiven, just as we are, should be comforting to all of us.

A Critique of the "Healing Cult" within the Christian Tradition

The "healing cult" that has developed in the Christian tradition distorts and misinterprets the relationship between faith and healing described in the disability passages. The way people with disabilities have been treated under the guise of faith healing is nothing short of religious abuse.

This healing cult has a long, grim history in Christianity. In the early fourteenth century, Blessed Margaret of Castello, a woman with multiple disabilities, was taken to faith healers by her aristocratic parents at the age of fourteen. When she was not healed, they abandoned her far from home and never saw her again. She became a lay Dominican, known for her works of mercy and extraordinary faith. Today, her body lies incorrupt in the Dominican church in Città de Castello, Italy, as her cause for canonization progresses.

Theologian and disability advocate Nancy Eiesland tells of her personal experience with faith healing. As a small child, she was given mixed messages about her disability. She was taken to faith healers and prayed over expectantly. "My family frequented faith healers with me in tow. I was never healed. People asked about my hidden sins, but they must have been so hidden that they were misplaced by even me."[40] She was also told that God gave her a disability to develop her character. "By the age of six or seven, I was convinced that I had enough character to last a lifetime."[41] These two conflicting messages must have been very confusing to a small child.

Faith healers and TV evangelists, even well-intentioned ones, who prey on vulnerable people telling them that their faith will heal them are doing a terrible injustice to these people, and to the Christian community, as well as distorting the purpose and meaning of the healing narratives. I am certain that Jesus Christ did not intend for a huge cult focused only on physical cures to develop as a result of his relationships with some thirteen disabled people. The subject of why Jesus was in relationship with people with disabilities is explored in a more comprehensive way in part III.

The Human Jesus and the Risen Christ: Disabled and Proud of It

Finally, one of the last things that happened to Jesus before he died was to become disabled. The nail wounds in both his hands and his feet would have caused permanent damage to his tendons and ligaments, probably limiting his ability to use his hands as well as walk and stand for long periods of time. In the absolute perfection of the resurrection, Jesus was not stripped of disabilities and scars. Indeed, not only were they still present, they were one of the ways he identified himself to others. "Look at my hands and my feet, see that it is I myself. And when he had said this, he showed them his hands and feet."[42] He even allowed his scars to be touched. "Then He said to Thomas, 'Put your finger here and see my hands. Reach out your hand and put it in my side.' "[43] He showed his scars openly and without shame for they were, and remain, a sign of his humanity and the fullness of his life experience.

The Problem of the Connection between Disability and Sin

As he walked along, he saw a man blind from birth. His disciples asked him, "Rabbi, who sinned, this man or his parents, that he was born blind?" Jesus answered, "Neither this man nor his parents sinned; he was born blind so that God's work might be manifest in him. We must work the works of the one who sent me while it is day; night is coming when no one can work. As long as I am in the world, I am the light of the world. When he had said this, he spat on the ground and made mud with the saliva and spread the mud on the man's eyes saying to him, "Go wash in the pool of Siloam" (which means Sent). Then he went and washed and came back able to see.

John 9: 1–41

Widely recognized as one of the masterpieces of Johannine storytelling, the story of the "man born blind" is intense, multivalent, and fertile with Christological and theological meaning.[44] It is also troubling for people with disabilities in that it makes a connection between disability and sin. This connection has a long history in both the Hebrew Scriptures and the New Testament. A variety of meanings and interpretations have been assigned to this concept which have translated into very harmful realities for people with disabilities. The insinuation that a moral transgression is the cause of a disability must be challenged, for it suggests that people with disabilities are inferior and results in exclusion on many levels. Even though Jesus clearly refutes the idea, this connection is still made. One need only consult many of the leading biblical commentaries to find remarks that indicate a deep bias against the disabled person. For example, Gerald Sloyan comments on "the making of an imperfect newborn child."[45] *The Interpreter's Bible* says, "A whole man would have been no use to Christ"[46] (as if anyone is whole). People with disabilities are constantly being referred to as "afflicted," "broken," "poor," and by other pejorative or derogatory terms. These terms expose and perpetrate biases that are dangerous and continue to cause suffering, alienation, isolation, and shame in the lives of people with disabilities and their families. A challenge and reinterpretation is needed. To do so, I pursue three questions. First, who is this man? Second, what prompted the disciple's question: *"Rabbi, who sinned, this man or his parents, that he was born blind?"* And, third, What is the meaning of Jesus' answer: *"Neither this man nor his parents sinned; he was born blind so that God's work might be manifest in him"*?

Who is this man? Like almost all of the people with disabilities in the Gospels, the man does not have a name, which renders him without status in the ancient world. He is merely an object of the seeing world. He differs from many other people with disabilities in the Gospel in that he does not ask for healing. He is a beggar, a common occupation for a disabled person in the first century and, indeed, in the twenty-first. The "blind man" begging or selling pencils is a sight with which we are all still familiar, for even today 66 percent of people with disabilities are unemployed. He is, however, an intelligent and articulate man for he stands up to a series of intense and pointed questions about his experience of being healed and the identity of Jesus, first from his neighbors and then from the Pharisees, before being expelled from the temple twice. Although he may have been somewhat overwhelmed and disoriented by the bright light and first sights, he remains in control. He is not easily intimidated and even has a sense of humor. Raymond Brown calls the blind man clever and voluble.[47] Colleen Grant describes him not simply "as a broken figure in need of compassion and healing but as a person in his own right. We are able to get to know him as a thoughtful, brave, amusing, but above all, ordinary person."[48]

What prompted the disciple's question: *"Rabbi, who sinned, this man or his parents, that he was born blind?"* Many scholars claim that the notion that sin, by whomsoever committed, was the cause of blindness and other disabilities was common thinking in first-century Jerusalem. Rudolf Bultmann believes that the disciple's question assumes certain well-known views at the time, such as illness being thought of as a punishment for one's own sins, and the idea that the parents' guilt was punished in their children. He calls these ideas universal in the ancient world.[49] Taken, then, in an historical context, this is not a controversial or inflammatory question.

In his response, Jesus, as he often does, departs from the

thinking of his time. He quickly and clearly refutes the idea that the man's blindness is because of his sin or the sins of his parents. *"Neither this man nor his parents sinned."* He goes on to suggest there is another way of looking at this situation. What is the meaning of the second part of the answer Jesus gives: *"so that God's work might be manifest in him"?* Jesus deals with the particular case in question by naming the purpose of the man's blindness as an opportunity to make God's work visible in him. The common interpretation tends to make the point that it is the removal of his blindness that is the manifestation of God's work. Again, as in many other passages, the removal of the disability is used as a method of Christological identification.

This brief dialogue is most likely a literary device used to move the story along and to develop and reveal theological and Christological meaning. It, nonetheless, does make an unfortunate connection between sin and disability. This notion has contributed to the marginalization of people with disabilities. The fruits of the thinking that connects disability with sin have lead to a history of disability filled with shame, despair, loneliness, and alienation. If we are serious about inclusion of people with disabilities, these perceptions must be challenged.

How is this to be done? Perhaps our search begins with a series of pointed questions, not unlike the questions that were fired at the man in this Gospel passage:

- What are our stereotypes and perceptions about people with disabilities?
- Do we secretly wonder if maybe they did do something wrong?
- Do we feel superior to people with disabilities?
- Do we patronize them? Do we pity them?
- Do we see only their disabilities, not their abilities?

The man in this Gospel story breaks many of the stereotypes about people with disabilities. He is smart, clever, tenacious, and boldly speaks out, identifying and defending Jesus. He names Jesus as a prophet, and in doing so becomes a prophet himself.

- Do we really want to include those who have been rendered "other" by society?
- Are we willing to make accommodations and commit time and resources to make our communities available to one another?

Understanding the Johannine community that is the backdrop for this story is helpful, for it can be seen as a model of inclusivity where pluralism was accepted and celebrated. The Johannine understanding of sin as "the result of failure in the face of justice and confrontation which brings Christ to the world"[50] can be readily applied to this topic.

And finally, can we accept that we cut ourselves off from seeing and experiencing how the works of God are manifest if we choose not to engage with our brothers and sisters with disabilities? Can we acknowledge that the way God's work may be manifest in us is through the way we relate to those who are oppressed by society? For we are only given the privilege to "work the works of God" when we are inclusive within our own communities.

The Problem of Access to Liturgy and the Sacraments

An Imaginary Assembly

The sanctuary is lovely. The altar has been lovingly decorated; candles ready to be lighted; gifts of bread and wine laid out with respect and love prepared for the entire congregation to receive the Eucharist in both species. The pastor has spent hours preparing a homily that ties together God's Words and has meaning to the congregation. Lay readers, eucharistic ministers, and altar girls and boys have been properly prepared for their respective roles. The fairly paid music ministers have selected music that perfectly coordinates with the readings and a well rehearsed choir stands ready to lead the assembly in song. The people of God arrive early to make sure they get a parking space and a place to sit. They walk up the stairs and are greeted at the door by the Hospitality Committee. Smiles, nods, and hugs are exchanged as they find a seat, genuflecting as they enter the pew. It is quiet and peaceful; maybe even awesome and dignified. As members of the assembly, those gathered intuitively understand their connectedness to each other and to Christians who have gathered, for almost two thousand years, in historically different but intentionally similar assemblies to celebrate the most amazing gift in the history of the world: Jesus' gift of himself, to us, in the Eucharistic celebration.

A Harris survey commissioned by the National Organization on Disability in 1994 reported that 68 percent of people with disabilities consider their religious faith to be "very important." Overall attendance at religious services is about 10 percentage points less for people with disabilities than for the nondisabled population, but people with disabilities are nearly twice as likely (39 percent to 22 percent) never to participate in religious services.[51] These statistics are revealing and alarming. While the percentage of people who consider their religious faith important is higher than the general population, participation in an assembly setting is lower. Don Saliers calls liturgy "a school for compassion—not pity, not sympathy—but compassion. It is about being companions, breaking bread together signifying that we're willing to weep with those who weep and rejoice with those who rejoice. Such compassion abides in the heart of God."[52] Saliers goes on to say that "The spiritual pulse and the gifts people with disabilities bring to churches and synagogues—a way of seeing things long obscured and neglected—raises important theological and spiritual questions about the nature and quality of our worshiping assemblies."[53] What do our assemblies look like? Are they schools of compassion? Many people with disabilities would claim they are not.

Gordon Lathrop, in *Holy Things*, describes this gathered church—the assembly—as "people gathered around certain central things, and these things, by their juxtapositions, speaking truly of God and suggesting a meaning for all things."[54] Lathrop asserts the primacy of the assembly when he asks: "What do you need a church for? People, of course. People are primary. The Church is an assembly of people."[55]

And yet, if we, who love and are the Christian community, search our assemblies with truth and care, we must face a serious reality. Some of the people of God are denied access to this assembly and these "certain central" things of God. Who among us is missing? How is this access to the holy things that speak of God denied? Where is Tim Jackman, who uses a wheelchair and can't get up those steps? Where is Mary Palmer, who is legally blind and can't read the bulletin? Where is Miguel Gonzalez, who has cerebral palsy and drools, maybe even in the Eucharistic cup? What about Tonya Robinski, who is mentally retarded and never been given the opportunity to receive the Eucharist? Where is Susie Heller, a person with mental illness, who looks somewhat disheveled and who, in her own words, is in one of her "bad" periods? What about Eric Bowman, who is a paraplegic as a result of a boating accident, attends Mass faithfully and harbors a secret yearning to be a priest, which he has never mentioned to anyone because he fears being rejected and ridiculed? Where is Barbara Mitchell, who is deaf and can't hear the joyful music or Father's well-prepared homily? Where is the Smith family and their two young autistic children?

People with disabilities often suffer from chronic exclusion: exclusion as a way of life. Not being able to get up the stairs to the church where your daughter is being married. Attending an all-day RCIA Workshop and not being able to use the restroom in the parish hall. Not being able to read the bulletin or hear the homily. Being at home without accessible transportation the night of the Easter Vigil when your best friend is being welcomed into the church. Being embarrassed to go up the aisle to communion because it takes you so long using your walker. Being just discharged from a two-week stay in a psychiatric hospital and going to church hoping to find a welcoming community of faith and not having anyone even say hello. Not being able to receive the sacrament of penance because you are unable to communicate through speech. Being told you cannot receive the Eucharist because "you won't understand" what you are doing.

Lack of access to the sacraments for people with both developmental and physical disabilities can be easily documented. In *Developmental Disabilities and Sacramental Access*, Mary Therese Harrington explains that people with mental retardation or other developmental disabilities are frequently refused access to the sacraments in the Catholic Church. Edward Foley, OFM Cap., tells of being "stunned by the revelation and Mary Therese's calm when she spoke of it."[56] It is, however, quite commonplace. I personally know several couples with developmental disabilities that have enjoyed long, happy marriages, although Father Foley notes in his book that there was an "inability even to begin addressing the question of sacramental marriage for those with developmental disabilities."[57] People with physical disabilities tell of being denied the sacrament of marriage because of their inability to conceive a child by traditional means. Until only recently, canon law denied the sacrament of holy orders to people with certain types of disabilities. Without belaboring the point further with more painful examples, it is easy to see how people with disabilities are excluded from the liturgical and sacramental life of the church.

In the Roman Catholic tradition, *Sacrosanctum Concilium*, "The Constitution on the Sacred Liturgy," the first document promulgated by the Second Vatican Council, reveals a strong affirmation of the centrality of liturgical celebration when it states:

(1) . . . the liturgy is the summit toward which the activity of the Church is directed; at the same time it is the font from which all the Church's power flows.[58]

(2) . . . every liturgical celebration, because it is an action of Christ the priest, and of his Body which is the Church, is a sacred action

surpassing all others; no other action of the Church can equal its effectiveness.[59]

(3) The Church earnestly desires that all the faithful be led to that full, conscious and active participation in liturgical celebrations called for by the very nature of the liturgy. Such participation . . . is their right and duty by reason of their baptism. . . . for it is the primary and indispensable source from which the faithful are to derive the true Christian spirit.[60]

Words and concepts like "primary," "indispensable," "summit," "source," "font," and "sacred action surpassing all others" leave little room for interpretation. They proclaim, loudly and clearly, the centrality of liturgical celebration. Other Christian traditions also speak to the centrality of liturgical worship through pastoral documents and statements and ongoing practices. The idea of exclusion is always troublesome, but if one accepts the centrality of liturgical worship within the Christian community, then exclusion from liturgical worship becomes a serious and devastating spiritual and institutional problem. It is a rejection "surpassing all others," for from a spiritual perspective, what could be worse than to be excluded from the Lord's table? What could be worse than to be denied the bread of life and the cup of salvation?

These statements of centrality make the issue of exclusion of any of the faithful a situation with perilous consequences for all who exclude and are excluded. Those who participate in actions that deny access, intentionally or unintentionally, bear a heavy burden. And those who are denied access to their primary and rightful place in the assembly and at the Lord's table come to know a type of exclusion that is searing and devastating.

Writing in the "Amen Corner" of *Worship* magazine, Nathan Mitchell says, "It is both pastorally and theologically imperative that the Sunday assembly be—or become—a place where all the baptized faithful can find a home, can be welcomed as full members of the parish."[61]

What happens to those who are excluded? Certainly those of us who gather as community to meet our own spiritual needs prefer not to think about what happens to the people who are excluded or imagine how they might feel, particularly when we are not sure what we should do to become more inclusive. However, we must think about it. We must reflect on the consequences of our exclusivity.

Those excluded are effectively rendered assembly-less, Eucharist-less, and sacrament-less. Lathrop's holy things—bread, wine, water, book—are literally placed out of reach. Of course, those excluded are not rendered faith-less or spiritual-less. They set forth on their own spiritual and interior journeys to search for God. Where do these exclusion-driven journeys take them? Many leave, humiliated, angry, and in pain. They find other more welcoming Christian or non-Christian communities. They become secular humanists or virtuous pagans, and, in a secret place in their hearts, they remember their exclusion from the community that was supposed to be their spiritual home. Others remain on what we call the "fringe," actively involved in good works and personal devotions creating their own access to holy things. We must remember, too, that many people with disabilities are often economically disadvantaged and trapped in a vicious cycle of poverty and disability. They do not have the luxury of being secular humanists, doing good works, or even pausing to reflect on their exclusion. Their lives, though filled with hardships, are often quite spiritual, characterized by humility and vulnerability. Being with them often reminds others of God.

However meaningful or spiritual other activities are, Mitchell rightly asserts that "Christian life begins and ends at the table: the table of the baptismal Eucharist, the table of the farewell meal of a Christian in the liturgy of death and burial. We begin to live and we begin to die in that corporate assembly among whom Jesus Christ eats and drinks now that he is risen from the dead."[62] It is the marginalized Christian, indeed, who is excluded from the liturgy and the sacraments. Access to the liturgical and sacramental life of the church begins with "God's graciousness, not with human capacities, and relies upon the interdependence and openness of a community"[63]—openness in a community of believers such as the one in this re-imagined assembly.

The sanctuary is lovely. The aisles are wide, and pews interspersed throughout the church have been shortened to accommodate wheelchairs and walkers. The altar has been lovingly decorated; candles ready to be lit; care has been taken to include sensory stimuli for people who don't process information in the traditional way. Gifts of bread and wine are laid out with respect and love prepared for the entire congregation to receive the Eucharist in both species. The pastor, who has cerebral palsy and is unable to speak, has spent hours preparing a homily that ties together God's Words and has meaning to the congregation. His homily will be preached with the assistance of his Liberator, his state-of-the-art assistive technology device. No one will fail to understand the metaphors of liberation that the priest and his Liberator suggest. Lay readers, eucharistic ministers, and altar girls and boys have been properly prepared for their respective roles. They include an older woman with mental illness, a man with MS, and a young man who uses a wheelchair. One of the altar boys has Down syndrome. The music ministers have selected music that perfectly coordinates with the readings and a well-rehearsed choir stands ready to lead the assembly in song. An interpreter is in place for those members of the community who are deaf. Copies of the bulletin have been printed in large type for those with visual impairments. The people of God arrive early to make sure they get a parking space and a place to sit. There is adequate handicap parking and adapted transportation available. All entering pass a big sign outside welcoming all including people with disabilities. They walk up the stairs or wheel up the ramp, and are greeted at the door by the Hospitality Committee, an older man and his thirty-year-old daughter who is mentally retarded. Smiles, nods, and hugs are exchanged as they find a seat, genuflecting, if they are able, as they enter the pew. It is quiet and peaceful, maybe even awesome and dignified. As members of the assembly, those gathered intuitively understand their connectedness to each other and to Christians who have gathered, for almost two thousand years, in historically different but intentionally similar assemblies to celebrate the most amazing gift in the history of the world: Jesus' gift of himself, to us, in the Eucharistic celebration. Using his electric wheelchair, Father starts slowly up the aisle as the choir leads the congregation in singing "We Are the Body of Christ."

A fantasy? An impossibility? Or a joyful, mysterious "come as you are"[64] party where all are welcomed to a school of compassion, hope, and promise?

Why a Theology of Access?

Indeed the body does not consist of one member, but many. There are many members, yet one body. The eye can not say to the hand, "I have no need of you," nor the head to the feet, "I have no need of you." On the contrary, the members of the body that seem to be the weakest are indispensable.

1 Corinthians 12: 20–22

In this part, I examined the Christian tradition from the perspective of the contemporary disability movement with the express intention of using these insights to develop a theology of access for people with disabilities. The purpose of the theology of access that I am proposing is the inclusion of people with disabilities in the Body of Christ. That Body, as we know it, is pneumatological, sacramental, and ecclesiological. The church, under the guidance of the Holy Spirit, should provide a liberatory access to all and should be the showplace of God's love, mercy, and compassion. Why a theology of access? Because the gospel of Jesus Christ is a gospel of access; creating access for those on the margins is a Christian mandate. Because access is, as I stated in the introduction, a mystical and moral matter.

All of us have been excluded at one time or another in our

life. It is a painful experience that hurts us deeply. Usually our experiences of exclusion are occasional and balanced by a sense of belonging to the various groups that give our lives a context. People with disabilities, however, often suffer from chronic exclusion, exclusion as a way of life.

Quite simply, people with disabilities have been, and are still, in large measure, excluded and marginalized within the Christian tradition. Deborah Creamer, writing in the *Journal of Religion in Disability and Rehabilitation*, explains the experiences of people with disabilities:

> In discussing religion and disability, we are first confronted by the problem of access. Simply put, people with disabilities are constantly confronted by barriers that deny their access to many areas of life. This problem is of concern to us for two reasons: first, it is a question of justice, and second, people with disabilities are barred from full participation in the church, theological education and ministry and theology as professions. . . . We cannot spend time discussing our understandings of God and Christ when we are struggling to feed ourselves because no one will hire us. Accessibility issues are the most pressing concern for most disabled people.[65]

Lack of access for people with disabilities impacts on the meaning of the church and its institutional and sacramental life. Gordon Lathrop says that "The manner of our access to holy things has everything to do with their meaning. Access to the meeting may be the primary locus for the theology of the meeting."[66] The identity and mission of the church are explicitly tied to who is present and who is absent.

Fears, prejudices, ignorance, and apathy toward people who are disabled or others who are marginalized by society narrows the ability of the church to respond to its mission, for "it is in the loving union of believers in Christ which seeks out the least of the brethren [sic] and excludes no one, that most fundamentally reveals the glory of God in Christ. . . . This loving union is proper to the person of the Spirit and is the Spirit's final goal and greatest work."[67]

Lathrop refers to the church as a "holy circle" that is not holy enough and a "sacred assembly" that is not wide enough. He reminds us that the "ordo requires all sacred things to face their failures. After all, the center of this circle and the meaning of the ordo is Jesus Christ, the one who is always identified with the outsider."[68]

And so, we stand ready to face our failures. We want to widen the circle. But how do we go about it? The acknowledgment that our attitudes and actions have excluded people is the place to begin. One of the hallmarks of the parousia will be that no one will be excluded. All of God's people will experience a sense of belonging as margins cease to exist. The circles of assemblies we call "church" will have boundaries that are easily accessed. The overflowing and crowded margins filled with the left-outs and the left-overs, the misfits, the poor, and the estranged will integrate with those comfortably situated in the center who, of course, in spite of their appearances of comfort and belonging are no strangers to marginality. Until that day arrives, we must continue to strive, in our imperfect and limited ways, to become church and to build an inclusive kingdom on earth.

A theology of access acknowledges that our commitment to inclusion is not because we are being generous or good Christians, but because it is a gospel mandate. A theology of access demands that we accept that God is not accessible to us on our own terms, and that making a place and a space for others, even and especially "people of exclusion," is one of the basic requirements of the Christian life. A theology of access demands we search our community with truth and face the serious reality that some of the people of God have been systematically denied access to the community. A theology of access demands that we admit that our own attitudes and actions have excluded people. It forces us to ask difficult questions. How can we become more inclusive? What actions do we need to take? What skills do we need? How must we change to make this gospel demand a reality in our communities? Becoming inclusive is a complex, demanding task that asks more of us than we are probably willing to give. It requires the traits of patience and vigilance that are in short supply in our fast-paced, outcome-oriented world. And yet, we cannot be faithful to our Christian vocation if we are not serious about the Christian mandate for inclusion.

Are Access and Inclusion Possible?

Any serious discussion of inclusion must include a reflection on the challenges, struggles, and limits of inclusion. The realities of the demands on the community must be named. It is not surprising that there is a systematic tendency toward excluding people with disabilities or others who do not fit within the fairly clear and tight boundaries of cultural norms. The one who is different—in this case, the one who cannot walk, the one who cannot hear, the one with altered speech or mannerism, the one who demands a rethinking of what it means to be human and what it means to be beautiful—asks a great deal of us. We are asked to think, to look and to see, to listen, to slow down, to face the ways we ourselves are different, to extend ourselves, and, ultimately, to change. No wonder inclusivity is a real struggle.

The topic of inclusivity/exclusivity within the theological conversation is not without its own paradoxes for this is surely the most inclusive time in the history of theology. I believe that history will remember the twentieth century for this inclusivity: as the time when the pivotal role of men in the European universities (invariably clerics) diminished and diverse voices, almost all previously excluded, not only joined but also influenced and changed the theological conversation. These intense, sometimes dissonant, and often pained voices paved the way for discussions on many topics that were formerly ignored or unacknowledged. Bringing topics like oppression, access, and inclusion to dialogue can be difficult, dangerous, frightening. How do we, as Paul says, "Go forward on the road that has brought us to where we are"? How do we negotiate a road with few landmarks, rocky terrain, unfamiliar landscape? Nathan Mitchell challenges us when he says, "The real test of Church is whether it can make room for difference, for diversity, for the left-out and the left-over, for the marginal, for the stranger and the estranged."[69] In an interesting way, people with disabilities become the metaphor that shocks us into seeing our exclusionary patterns. A living metaphor—a flesh and blood, embodied metaphor—that challenges our attitudes, makes us face our fears, our prejudices, and our apathy. Considering our exclusionary patterns cannot help but make us uncomfortable.

The practical realities of inclusion are daunting. We are first asked to consider who we are and what we stand for. We will be asked to redefine our theologies and ministries. We will be asked to redefine ministry in general, as we broaden our understanding of participation and make room for others who will probably do things very differently than we are accustomed. Inclusion will strain our limited financial and human resources. The elimination of architectural barriers will be required and we will have to learn about assistive technology and adaptive equipment. And we will be asked to develop new models of hospitality that take us places we would probably rather not go. Such is the gospel mandate. Such is being in relationship with the radical love of the Father, Son, and Holy Spirit.

Our pluralistic and ambiguous world begs some difficult, but valid, questions. Are access and inclusivity even possible in the twentieth-first century? If so, what are the limits of inclusivity? What are the responsibilities of those who seek access? How much can we give? How much can we be asked to change? How much can we burden our already overburdened structures? How much can we stretch our already overstretched financial and human resources? What if welcoming the stranger—in this case, the person with a disability—changes what we have beyond recognition or intelligibility? Can we throw open the doors without becoming completely overwhelmed, without losing everything we value and love? These difficult questions certainly need to be considered. And yet, Lathrop brings us to a different reality when he says:

> First of all, we need to acknowledge that we are ourselves the persons requiring formation, reconciliation, and entrance rites. We are the strangers. This is so not only because of the general modern insight that everyone always feel like the outsider in any group: part of the individual self remains unrevealed: one is always, at least partly, excluded; one's attempts at acting included are often largely denial or pretense. This is so, but in Christian use, this insight is given a theological home. At the center of our meeting, is the one who always stands with the outsiders, the uninvited, the godless.[70]

And so as Christians, poised at the beginning of a new millennium, in what many would call the post-Christian era, we must ask ourselves, where do we stand? And with whom do we stand? And just how much are we willing to extend ourselves?

PART III

A THEOLOGY OF ACCESS

EIGHT

~

God's Love and Mercy: Altogether Inclusive

In Jesus Christ, God heals divisions, reconciles the alienated, gives hope to those who have none, offers forgiveness to the sinner, includes the outcast. In the end, God's love and mercy are altogether inclusive, accepting the repentant master as well as the repentant slave. If anyone were to be ultimately excluded from the reign of God it would be because he or she had set himself or herself as the final criterion of who should be included in God's reign. Still, the exclusion of even a single person is contrary to God's providential plan.[1]

Catherine La Cugna
God for Us: The Trinity and Christian Life

Conceiving the Trinity and the Church in Terms of Access

How are God, Jesus Christ, the Holy Spirit, and the church to be conceived to fulfill God's providential plan for inclusion? In part II, I presented a discussion of six theological topics from a

129

disability perspective with the intent of challenging and inform-
ing the Christian community. These ideas form the foundational thinking for the theology of access I present in this
section, and where I call for:

1. an all-encompassing Christian anthropology
2. an inclusive theology of embodiment
3. an analysis of the disability Scripture passages using a
   new way of thinking
4. inclusion in the core experience of the community's liturgical and sacramental life
5. a meditation on the relationship between disability and
   spirituality
6. a response to the injustice of the oppression of people with
   disabilities.

The theology of access I propose incorporates these concepts
and moves beyond them to develop a broader understanding of
how access can be created within the Christian community. It
is built upon the three-part God: Father, Son, and Holy Spirit,
acknowledging that a life of love and communion with others
where inclusion is the rule, not the exception, can only be realized in a Trinitarian context. It is theological, in that it is organized around theological categories, and it is practical, in that it
makes many concrete suggestions on inclusive practices.

The theological categories used are Christology, pneumatology, ecclesiology, spirituality, and morality as explicated in the
following topics:

1. Jesus Christ: God's Copious Gift
2. A Relational Christology: Toward a Ministry of Access
3. The Holy Spirit: A Model of Inclusion
4. The Church: A Model for an Accessible Community
5. Beyond Access: A Spirituality of Friendship

6. Human Vulnerability: Source of Communion in the Kingdom

The practical categories all focus on ways to offer access to people with disabilities and are organized under the following topics:

1. How to Develop Inclusive Practices
2. Responsibilities of Religious Leaders
3. Disability Etiquette
4. Architectural Barriers
5. Inclusive Language
6. Preaching
7. "Church Place Accommodations"—Using Technology
8. Access to Ministerial Leadership

Jesus Christ: God's Copious Gift

A theology of access is grounded in the concrete reality that God sent his only child to enter into the frailty and vulnerability of human life to offer all of humanity the gift of salvation and the opportunity for life with God. Edward Schillebeeckx, in his epic *Jesus: An Experiment in Christology* describes "Jesus as host: a copious gift of God."[2] For Schillebeeckx Jesus is "God's eschatological messenger, conveying the news of God's invitation to all—including and especially those officially regarded as outcasts."[3] If Jesus is God's eschatological messenger, sent to bring hope to the world, then what it means to model Jesus, is to be, if you will, an "eschatologist," that is, a hope giver. The social location for the promised wellspring of Christian hope is a community of believers who share life in a very particular way. This way, a "trinitarian faith,"[4] as LaCugna calls it, means "living for God."[5] The community of believers, then, comes together in a highly intentional manner, seeking a life that is "from and for

God, and from and for others."[6] To live for God means that we emulate the way Jesus Christ lived, preaching the Good News, relying totally on God, and giving ourselves over to the power and presence of the Holy Spirit. When we live for God, in Christ, through the power of the Holy Spirit, we cannot help but give hope to others, and we cannot help but be inclusive. The gospel of Jesus Christ is a call to a new world order where outsiders become insiders. The church as the Body of Christ is the quintessential inclusive community, where Jesus Christ, the one who is always identified with the outsider, presides as the copious host. We are called, through our baptism, to be his co-hosts. Co-hosting the party to bring about the Kingdom of God, in the here and now, is all about making room for the "other." As copious hosts, we are called to make God's love and mercy a palpable, tangible reality in the Christian community and in the world. Copious hosting demands we venture beyond the familiar and extend ourselves to others in faith and love. The rest of this book is devoted to articulating a theory and a praxis of copious hosting to people with disabilities. It begins, of course, with God's copious gift, Jesus, the one who always stands with the outsider.

Attempting to figure out who Jesus was, why he was sent, and what he was doing has dominated Christian thought for two thousand years. Numerous possibilities have been suggested to answer these complicated and multivalent questions. Specific questions that relate directly to a theology of access are: Why was Jesus actively involved with people with disabilities throughout his ministry? What do these relationships reveal to us about Jesus? About the Reign of God? About how we are to act with each other as we work to build the Kingdom of God Jesus preached? About how to live by faith discipleship?

A theology of access proposes a relational Christology. This Christology looks at Jesus in relationship, first, with people with disabilities, in general, and then with Bartimaeus, a man with a disability. I suggest the interactions in these relationships are a blueprint for copious hosting in the Christian community.

A Relational Christology:
Toward a Ministry of Access

"Stand up, take your bed, and go to your home."

Matthew 9:6

Then he touched their eyes and said, "According to your faith, let it be done."

Matthew 9:29

Then he said to the man, "Stretch out your hand."

Matthew 12:13

Jesus touched their eyes.

Matthew 20: 34

He took him aside in private, away from the crowd, and put his fingers in his ears, and he spat and touched his tongue.

Mark 7:33

As mentioned in part II, one of the reasons why Jesus was probably drawn to people with disabilities is because they were marginalized, and Jesus understood his place to be with those who were outcasts. To people with disabilities, and others who were marginalized, he was the copious host. All throughout the Scriptures, Jesus' ministry is marked by an unwavering commitment to access and inclusion. He singles out people with disabilities and recognizes their great faith. He chooses people with disabilities to assist in revealing his identity. He is keenly aware of the marginalization of people with disabilities and seeks to change their situations. His interest reveals his compassion. He responds differently to each individual situation. He uses different methods of healing depending on the situation and needs and personality of the particular person, and these methods often include physical contact. It is noteworthy that

Jesus was not afraid of physical intimacy with people with disabilities, although this surely would have been frowned on in his culture.

Jesus was not a magician or a miracle worker. He was, and is, God. Although he could have, he did not heal every disability. He did not want or need to, because Jesus was not afraid of human frailty. Quite the contrary. He did not cling to Godliness. He entered fully into the human condition, embraced the frailty of life, and was vulnerable, even unto death.

I now consider the relationship between Jesus and Bartimaeus, paying particular attention to how they act toward each other. Their interactions explain best the relational Christology that I argue is an excellent model for relationality within the Christian community.

Jesus and Bartimaeus

Bartimaeus . . . a blind beggar, was sitting on the roadside. When he heard it was Jesus of Nazareth, he began to shout out and say, "Jesus, Son of David, have mercy on me!" Many sternly ordered him to be quiet, but he cried out even more loudly, "Son of David, have mercy on me." Jesus stood still and said, "Call him here." And they called the blind man, saying to him. "Take heart; get up, he is calling you." So throwing off his cloak, he sprang up and came to Jesus. Then Jesus said to him, "What do you want me to do for you?" The blind man said to him, "My teacher, let me see again." Jesus said to him, "Go, your faith has made you well." Immediately he regained his sight and followed him on the way.

Mark 10: 48–52

The passage opens with the description of Bartimaeus, a blind beggar sitting on the roadside calling to Jesus. *"Many sternly ordered him to be quiet."* The crowd treats Bartimaeus in a disrespectful and demeaning way, sternly ordering him to be quiet. Scholars suggest the reason why the crowd speaks so harshly to Bartimaeus is "because they wished to hear Jesus"[7]; however, their rude treatment of him should not be so easily dismissed. Bartimaeus, however, is persistent. He cries out even more loudly in spite of the admonishments of the crowd: *"Have mercy on me."* Jesus, who was "passing by," responds to the cry of Bartimaeus. He stops walking and stands still when he hears the call of someone in need.

There is a dramatic change in the mood and behavior of the crowd when Jesus pays attention to Bartimaeus. "Call him here," Jesus tells the crowd. How quickly Jesus' exercise of authority turns things about.[8] Jesus steers the crowd away from exclusion. Including the crowd in this interchange is an act of great generosity on the part of Jesus, for he invites them to assist him, and in doing so, shows them the same mercy that Bartimaeus is seeking.

Bartimaeus throws off his cloak and runs to Jesus. The cloak was an outer garment similar to a cape or poncho that Bartimaeus probably used for multiple functions. By day, it was spread out in front of him to collect alms, and by night it was protection from the cold. People begging at the gates were probably a common sight.[9] It is likely that Bartimaeus was sitting on the edge of his cloak that was spread out in front of him when he heard that Jesus was approaching. Jacques Dupont makes the point that often this garment was the only protection that the poor had against the cold,[10] and it may well have been his only possession. Bartimaeus's immediate and enthusiastic response, indicated by the action verbs of "throwing off" and "sprang up," is touching especially because it involves leaving behind his only possession which was both his livelihood and his protection from the elements.

Jesus and Bartimaeus speak directly to each other. *"What do you want me to do for you?"* Bartimaeus responds substituting the royal "Son of David" with the more personal and respectful *"Rabonni,"* "my teacher." Jesus says, *"Go, your faith has made you well,"* ending Bartimaeus's blindness with words of salvation. Normally, Jesus performs some gesture or speaks a word when he accomplishes a miracle, but Jesus attributes this miracle to faith alone.[11] Robert Gundry points out that the word "go" may mean that Bartimaeus does not have to sit on the side of the road begging anymore.[12] This restores not only his sight but gives him access to a less marginalized life. This is the only miracle where someone follows Jesus.[13] Bartimaeus does this willingly and without prompting.

Who is this Bartimaeus? Is he a poor person with a life-altering disability being treated in an undignified way? A prophet without sight but with great vision? A marginalized beggar? The model of Christian discipleship? Many Scripture commentaries claim Bartimaeus sets the standard for Christian faith and discipleship. Fear consumed almost everyone else in Mark's Gospel but Bartimaeus, although poor and marginalized, was transformed by faith.

The story of Jesus and Bartimaeus is packed with action verbs—asking, telling, begging, rebuking, crying out, standing still, calling, throwing off, springing up, requesting, regaining, following. The Gospel of Mark, as Reynolds Price says, "lays its narrative bet upon described ACTION at the expense of conversation or monologue."[14] It is the actions in this story that describe the relational Christology I am proposing.

What Bartimaeus Does

- Expresses his need honestly and humbly.
- Is not deterred by those who call him away from faith.
- Even when provoked he does not respond negatively.
- Is willing to move quickly—to give up what he has to go to Jesus.
- Shows respect, familiarity, and love for Jesus.
- Is not afraid to approach Jesus.
- Knows that he is welcome to come to the Lord as evidenced by the title he uses to address Jesus (*Rabonni*). There is genuine warmth in their relationship.
- And, finally, he confidently follows Jesus with great trust, without knowing where they are going.

What Jesus Does

- Pays attention when he is called for help.
- Stops what he is doing and stands still.
- Listens in case he missed what was being said the first time.
- Directs his attention to the person who is calling him.
- Generously includes the community—in spite of the fact they were not behaving graciously—and shows them a different way of acting and interacting.
- Asks the person in need how he can help.
- And he gives without asking for anything in return.

What We Are to Do

How can we be copious hosts to one another? How can we model Jesus as a minister of access? We become the person we want to be by practicing the actions that reflect what it is we desire to become. In other words, we become the things we do. We become generous by being generous to others. We become kind by treating people kindly. We become copious hosts by copiously hosting.

Copious hosting begins with presence. Jesus and Bartimaeus were totally present to each other. Many years ago, I heard a homily where the preacher said, "Nothing makes a statement like your presence." Our presence reflects our intentions. Understanding that presence to each other, unadorned, without ceremony or fanfare, is not only enough, but is the essence of copious hosting is sometimes difficult in our fast-paced, outcome-oriented, technologically based, consumer-conscious, and media-driven world.

Copious hosts pay attention when they are called to or asked for help. They must be willing to stop what they are doing, be still, and listen carefully. Copious hosts direct full attention to the person in need. They are inclusive of the immediate community, even and especially when it may not be deserved. Copious hosts ask the person in need how they can help and respond by giving, graciously and generously, not expecting anything in return. Copious hosts know how to take as well as give. Copious hosts are humble and they allow their brothers and sisters a chance to be a copious host to them.

Copious hosts live by faith, trusting in God, depending on the power of the Holy Spirit, even when the future is unclear. Like Bartimaeus, they are not easily deterred or quickly discouraged. They seek what they need from God with a trusting heart. Copious hosts work to develop a familiar relationship with Jesus that is evidenced by constant contact and warmth. Like Bartimaeus, they call Jesus friend and teacher, and follow him with confidence.

The Holy Spirit: A Model of Inclusion

A theology of access offers new ways to understand the role of the Holy Spirit in the Christian life. Robert Schreiter believes that the Holy Spirit can be helpful "to come to terms with genuine pluralism as the Holy Spirit sets up a paradigm of inclusivity. At Pentecost, each was hearing God's message in their own language. The Holy Spirit has an element of the unexpected, the yet to be revealed, the surprise."[15] The Holy Spirit—radical love whirling through the universe—offers us great freedom to move beyond ourselves and extend ourselves to others.

From this perspective, the Holy Spirit offers great possibilities for access to people with disabilities in the following ways: (1) as marginalized companion; (2) as advocate; and (3) by providing unique points of ecclesiological entry. A brief consideration of each of these notions follows.

The Holy Spirit as Marginalized Companion

The Holy Spirit is the marginalized member of the Trinity. Elizabeth Johnson notes that, "In unusually colorful language, theologians today describe the Spirit as the forgotten God, something faceless, shadowy, ghostly, vague, the poor relation in the Trinity, the unknown or half-known God, even the Cinderella of theology."[16] Considering the fact that Jesus names the Spirit as God's eschatological gift, theology's neglect of the Holy Spirit is a scandal. Elizabeth Johnson agrees when she states:

> . . . what is being neglected is nothing less than the mystery of God's personal engagement with the world in its history of love and disaster; nothing less than God's empowering presence active within the cosmos from the beginning, throughout history, and to the end, calling forth life and freedom. Forgetting the Spirit is not ignoring a faceless, shadowy, third hypostasis but the mystery of God vivifying the world, closer to us than we are to ourselves, drawing near and passing by in liberating compassion.[17]

As the marginalized member of the Trinity, the Holy Spirit is meaningful to marginalized people. The Holy Spirit, as promised, is the God who is with us and for us, a companion who not only understands but also experiences marginalization. The Holy Spirit as eschatological gift empowers people with disabilities to take their rightful place in our midst and to become eschatological prophets themselves through the sharing of their experiences, and especially by their presence.

The Holy Spirit as Advocate

I shall ask the Father, and he will give you another Advocate
to be with you forever . . .

John 14:16

I have said all of these things to you while still with you:
but the Advocate, the Holy Spirit,
whom the Father will send in my name,
will teach you everything and
remind you of all I have said to you.

John 14:25–26

Advocacy is a central activity within the disability movement.[18] It is a word that has special and particular meaning to people with disabilities. A reinterpretation of these passages that correlates with a contemporary understanding of advocacy within the disability movement has the potential to be empowering to people with disabilities. A careful look at the meaning of "Advocate" as used by Jesus in these passages can be correlated with the empowerment of advocacy in the modern sense and experience. This can be explained through an understanding of three points.

First, the multiple meanings of the word *advocate*. The Greek word *paraklētos* (paraclete) used in the Johannine literature for both Jesus (1 Jn. 2:1) and the Spirit (14:26) seems to have meant "someone called in to help" (though not a professional attorney or lawyer). Sometimes, it seems to have had the sense of "comforter." The noun *paraklētos* is derived from the Greek verb *parakaleō*, which means to "exhort" or "comfort." The more general definitions of the word include supporter, helper, comforter, and advocate.[19]

Second, the understanding of the relationality between the disciples and the Spirit, as revealed in the Scriptures: D. Bruce Woll, in *Johannine Christianity in Conflict: Authority, Rank, Succession in the First Farewell Discourse*, makes this point when he says, "The authority of the disciples is grounded, finally, in the promise that 'another Paraclete' will be sent to dwell in them. What is new is the introduction of an active role for the disciples. In support of this suggestion we would call attention to the role of the disciples. It is they who are the viable successors of Jesus."[20] This active role given to the disciples is passed on to us and includes extending ourselves through copious hospitality. God's presence, revealed in the movement of the Holy Spirit, will always move toward inclusion.

Finally, the promises of the Spirit speak of an intimate, affective presence: Jesus promises that "the Spirit will come to dwell in them" (Jn. 14:23); "will lead them to truth" (Jn. 16:3); "will remind them of all Jesus told them" (Jn. 14:26); and "will be with them always" (Jn. 14:16) The notion of the "Holy Spirit as Advocate" correlates with a contemporary experience of advocacy, which is often an experience of support, help, comfort, relationality, and community. The promise of the Holy Spirit as Advocate, as helper, as comforter, as supporter, and as model of intimate, affective presence is a gift to the disability community.

The Holy Spirit as Point of Ecclesiological Entry

The Holy Spirit provides unique points of ecclesiological entry for people with disabilities. I suggest at least four: First, there is agreement with Elizabeth Johnson when she says "It may be that the amorphous character of the Spirit allows a particular openness to being appropriated in female images. . . ."[21] Similarly, it is likely that the neglect and marginalization of the Holy Spirit provides the very point of identification that allows entrance. Second, when Johnson notes that "The Spirit's presence through the praxis of freedom is often mediated amid profound ambiguity, often apprehended more in darkness than in light,"[22] it speaks to the experience of many people with disabilities. Most nondisabled people have no idea how difficult it is to have a disability and negotiate a world designed for nondisabled people. Third, the Holy Spirit points to relationality—to not only receiving but also giving—which provides the opportunity to both accept and contribute. Fourth, the multivalent and diverse nature of the Holy Spirit provides different ways of viewing the same thing, which is extremely significant for people whose whole life is an experience of being different.

The Church: A Model for an Accessible Community

When bars and supermarkets are more accessible than altars,
we all bear the shame.

Ginny Thornburgh

The Body of Christ presumes a place for everyone. The church fails in its mission if it is not an accessible, hospitable community. "Accessibility" is a buzzword in disability circles. Access to things like housing, employment, buildings, and community activities are one of the central demands of the disability movement. It is now time to ask this of the Christian community. Authentic accessibility is always grounded in both theory and practice. In other words, accessibility is both a way of thinking and a way of acting. The philosophical thinking that inspires authentic access has been explained in parts I and II of this book. The way of acting that reflects this thinking is explained throughout this chapter.

A number of suggestions are offered here for those who work to make Christ's church accessible. Some of these suggestions are reflective, some are pastoral, and some are practical. Some utilize traditional theological concepts; others enter into a more revolutionary realm. All reflect a commitment to full inclusion of people with disabilities. These suggestions are by no means exhaustive. Perhaps the best ideas are still to come as a result of personal commitments to inclusion and creative reflection in conversation with people with disabilities.

Nothing About Us Without Us[23]

One of the primary ways people with disabilities experience oppression is through domination by people who are not disabled, even well-intentioned family, friends, and professionals. People with disabilities tell of the common experience of being left out of the decision-making process on decisions that affect their lives. A theology of access calls for the participation of people with disabilities in making decisions that affect their lives. **Do not make decisions that affect people with disabilities without their participation.** We would never consider making decisions that affect a group of women or a group of Latinos without their participation, and yet it is common to find all types of planning done for people with disabilities without their input. For example, extensive remodeling with the express purpose of creating wheelchair access was recently completed in the chapel at the university where I work. An arbitrary decision was made to remove half of a row in a front pew of the church and half a row in a back pew of the church. No one thought to consult a person who uses a wheelchair! Consequently, the fact that there is no wheelchair access from the front door of the chapel was not addressed, the difficulties of negotiating the carpet were not addressed, and the fact that it is very difficult for a wheelchair to make the turn into the front pew was not discovered. Ask people with disabilities what they need and want. They will be your best resource for planning and make welcoming changes. Usually the best disability advocates are people with disabilities or their family members or friends. One of the reasons why Pope John Paul II held a worldwide conference on disability in 1988 was because one of his best friends became disabled. His experience with his friend was the catalyst for his becoming a disability advocate.

When making decisions, think in terms of the "Golden Rule of Community Inclusion: What Would You Do for Yourself?"[24] Would you like always to have to enter through the back door? Or always to have attention drawn to yourself by being singled out as "special"? Or to have to sit in the "handicapped" area away from your family and friends? Or be spoken about as if you were not present? Or to have someone decide what is best for you?

Do not be hesitant to communicate directly and frankly with people with disabilities on matters relating to their personal situations or situations affecting the entire community. Be prepared to listen to what they have to say, even if they offer a response that is not what you expect or desire. If you do not know people with disabilities that can help you, ask someone with a disability that worships in your community, or call a local advocacy organization, explain the issue that you are facing and ask for suggestions on who might assist you.

As church, we must boldly proclaim our desire to become more inclusive. Proclaiming the desire to be inclusive is powerful. Others, beyond the disability community, who also feel excluded will also be drawn to your community.

The universal pictorial sign for disability is rapidly moving toward becoming a multivalent symbol associated not just with physical access but as an inclusive welcome to all people with disabilities. There are also pictorial signs similar to the familiar wheelchair access sign for other types of disabilities. These symbols are readily available on most computer software programs under "symbols."

Christians should hang signs out in front of our churches that proclaim our welcome to people with disabilities. Signs should say something like "St. Dominic's welcomes people with disabilities and their families. Please call for assistance." A telephone and TTD number should be given and the universal symbols for disabilities should be displayed. Every bulletin, every week, in every church should have a similar message. People with disabilities should be encouraged to call and explain what type of accommodations they need to participate and every reasonable effort should be made to provide the accommodations.

Consider the needs of people with disabilities. For example, large print bibles should be available. At least one service a week should have signers available. Bulletins should be available in large type. Transportation is a common problem people with disabilities encounter, so a transportation network should be developed to ensure that rides are available to weekly services and special events.

Disability Etiquette

Sometimes nondisabled people are uncomfortable when meeting or interacting with a person with a disability because they are unsure of what to say or do. Obviously, ways to interact with a person with a disability varies depending on the nature and extent of the disability; however, there are some general guidelines that are helpful for successful interactions with people with disabilities.

- Use common sense. People with disabilities are just ordinary people and want to be treated in the same way you would like to be treated. Act in the same way you would normally act, appropriate to the situation at hand. Be relaxed. If you do something that you realize was not correct, just apologize and move on.
- Do not ask personal questions about someone's disability. If the person chooses to shares this information with you, react in a way that will communicate respect and support, not pity.
- Be careful that you do not unwittingly patronize a person with a disability. Patronization can occur in many forms such as treating the person as a child, discounting what they say, or making decisions for them.
- Always speak directly to the person with the disability, not to the person accompanying him or her.
- Be aware that a person with a disability sometimes needs extra time. Make this accommodation willingly in a way that does not make the person feel uncomfortable. Be willing to slow things down, allow a longer time for a restroom break, or to move from one location to another.
- It is fine to offer assistance, but always wait until your offer is accepted before you act. Ask for specific instructions if you are not sure what to do. If a person refuses assistance, do not be offended.
- Become familiar with the accessible facilities (restrooms, telephones, water fountains) where you work and worship, and share the information with people with disabilities. If there are any barriers that could be a problem, communicate this openly to anyone it might affect directly to avoid putting the person in an embarrassing situation.
- If you are planning a meeting or event, try to anticipate

what specific accommodations people with disabilities might need. Again, address potential barriers directly. If you know that individuals who use wheelchairs will be attending, arrange the clear space in advance.

- Do not park in accessible parking spaces or make jokes about people with disabilities getting all the good parking spaces.
- It is fine to use common expressions like "see you tomorrow" or "I've got to run now." What is not appropriate is to use disability slurs or descriptions that have negative meanings. A discussion on correct disability language is found later in this section.
- Use a normal tone of voice when speaking to a person with a disability. For some reason, people often tend to raise their voice when speaking to someone with a disability, although they are not necessarily hearing impaired. Do not raise your voice unless requested to do so.
- A smile along with a spoken greeting can be substituted for a handshake when deemed appropriate.
- Never touch a person with a disability in a familiar way unless you are on personal terms with him or her. I have seen people pat a person who uses a wheelchair on the head at their first meeting.
- If an individual uses a wheelchair, respect the wheelchair and space around it. Do not touch the wheelchair, or lean on it, or push it without being asked.
- If you are going to speak with an individual who uses a wheelchair for any period of time, it is best to sit at eye level.
- If an individual is blind or has a visual impairment, identify yourself and introduce others who are in the room, when greeting him or her, and do not leave the room without excusing yourself. In a group setting, speakers should identify themselves.
- If the person who is blind is unfamiliar with the room or the area, it is acceptable to ask if they would like a descrip-

tion of the layout and the furniture. If you do so, be specific and clear.

- If you are asked to guide someone with a sight disability, never push or pull the person. Allow him or her to take your arm, and walk slightly ahead so they can follow your body motions. Verbally point out stairs, doors, turns, and curbs as you approach them.
- Never pet or distract a guide dog. It is not a pet. This dog is responsible for its owner's safety and is always working. If you distract the dog, you could put the owner in jeopardy.
- Do not assume that all individuals who are blind read Braille. It is now common to also use voice-activated scanners, tape recorders, or other assistive technology.
- If an individual has a hearing impairment, it is acceptable to wave your hand or to tap the person gently on the shoulder to get their attention.
- Never pretend to understand what a person is saying. Listen attentively and be patient. It is fine to ask short questions that a nod or a yes or no will answer. It is fine to ask the person to repeat or rephrase, or offer a pen and paper.
- Some individuals who are deaf use American Sign Language. Be aware that this is not a universal language.
- If an individual who is deaf lipreads, you can help by looking directly at the person and speaking clearly, naturally, and slowly. Not all persons with hearing impairments can lipread. Those who do will rely on facial expression and other body language to help in understanding. Show consideration by placing yourself facing the light source and keeping your hands away from your mouth while speaking. Shouting does not help. Written notes can be useful.
- If an individual has a developmental disability, keep the communication direct and simple. Stay focused on the person and give them time to understand and answer. It may be helpful to repeat their answer for clarity. Do not talk to them as if they are a child, unless they are a child. Do not

assume that they don't have an opinion or good ideas and suggestions. You might be surprised by what they can offer to a group or conversation.

While these guidelines are not comprehensive, they should give you a good idea of some of the general and specific ways to create situations for successful interactions with people with different types of disabilities. Should you wish further information about a specific disability, consult *From Barriers to Bridges: A Community Action Guide for Congregations and People with Disabilities* by Janet Miller Rife and Ginny Thornburgh (Washington, D.C.: National Organization on Disability, 1996), or check on the many different web sites which offer good information on disability etiquette.

Responsibilities of Religious Leadership

Religious leaders bear a particular responsibility in this area for they set the tone for the entire community. If a leader is ignorant or insensitive to the needs of the disability community, then it is likely that this will be reflected in the wider community. Some of the ways to foster inclusion of people with disabilities include the following:

- Become knowledgeable about the different types of disabilities among the members of your own community, and offer the spiritual, moral, or physical supports that are needed to offer these individuals access.
- Be aware that when a member of your community becomes disabled, or has recently given birth to a child with a disability, they will need extra support. Do not wait for them to ask. Approach them and initiate conversation on an ongoing basis.
- Set up a "Committee on Disability Issues" to address a wide variety of disability related issues.

- Make sure that at least half the members of the committee are people with disabilities.
- Invite a disability advocate to provide training on the new paradigms in disability philosophy to the committee.
- Agenda items should include (a) the moral implications of exclusion; (b) the religious meaning of disability; (c) the barriers to participation that people with disabilities and their families might encounter in your community; (d) the physical access problems in buildings; (e) and how to attract and welcome those who are missing.
- Have an advocate for people with disabilities, preferably a person with a disability, as an ex-officio member of the pastoral council.
- Hire qualified people with disabilities.
- Include people with disabilities in a wide variety of volunteer leadership roles that are not just related to disability issues.
- Religious educators should integrate children with disabilities into their programs. Separate programs are not usually desirable.
- Religious educators should become familiar with and use a variety of strategies for teaching that include multi-sensory materials.
- Provide training to leaders of Bible Study groups on ways to interpret the disability Scriptures in an affirming way.
- Work with the music ministers to select songs that do not isolate or offend people with disabilities.
- Follow the guidelines suggested below for inclusive language and ways to preach the disability Scriptures.

Architectural Barriers

Architecture speaks loudly. Jan Robitscher makes the point that "The hospitality expressed in the architecture of sacred space is really a sacrament (outward sign) of the hospitality of the people who worship there."[25] There is a relationship between sacred space and practical realities. When I lecture on access, I always begin by asking if those present would have come today if they were not certain that they were going to be able to find a bathroom they could use. We are talking about the basics here. Not being able to enter a building, get a drink of water, or use the bathroom is a terrible violation of the dignity of a human person. The Americans with Disabilities Act (ADA) has sought to correct this problem in public facilities and businesses. Instead of complaining about the cost or the inconvenience, the Christian community should be doing everything in its power to make sure people with disabilities have physical access to the spaces where Christians gather. Anything less is a scandal.

Walk around and do an inventory of the place where you worship as well as the meeting and office space. Is there a telephone that can be accessed from a wheelchair? Is there a water fountain that can be accessed? Where do people who use wheelchairs sit in your church? Is the food on the buffet tables at social events placed out of reach for someone in a wheelchair? Is there carpet that is hard to negotiate? What about the steps? Just one little step is often too many steps for a walker or wheelchair. Making architectural changes takes time, planning, and resources. I can't tell you how many bathrooms I have seen that were supposed to be wheelchair accessible and were not. Problems such as not being able to clear the door, not having adequate turn space, not being able to close the door to the stall, not being able to reach sink, faucets, or soap and paper towels are all common problems. Sometimes precious financial resources are wasted when changes are not planned properly. Do not attempt any changes to physical spaces without consulting with an architect who is familiar with designing accessible spaces, and always include a person with a disability when planning architectural changes.

Inclusive Language

Inclusive language is an important issue in the church today. It is also an important issue within the disability community. The oppression of people with disabilities through language manifests itself in at least three ways.

First, people with disabilities are oppressed by many of the nouns and verbs used as descriptors. Words and phrases such as "hopelessly crippled, deformed, twisted, afflicted by, stricken with, invalid, and victim" tend to sensationalize and dramatize being disabled and contribute to rendering people with disabilities as "other." They are referred to by euphemistic terms like "different-abled," "physically challenged," "mentally different," and "partially sighted." All of these terms tend to objectify and perceive the person only in terms of their disability.

Second, people with disabilities are oppressed by the frequent use of disability slurs. Members of different minority groups are all familiar with particular derogatory or demeaning terms used to describe them, and most of the time we are horrified to hear pejorative terms used about a particular minority group. Disability slurs are another story, however. No one thinks twice when they hear terms like "retard," "spaz," or "lame," used as a descriptor of a person with a disability, or as a way to insult a person who is nondisabled.

Third, people with disabilities are oppressed by the use of disability terms to describe negative behaviors, characteristics, or situations. Expressions like "she can't see past her nose," "limping along," "when he gets back on his feet again," "the blind leading the blind," "love is blind," and "busier than a one-armed paperhanger" are all insulting to people with disabilities. Because someone does not have speech or cannot hear does not mean they are "deaf and dumb." A person is not "confined" to a wheelchair; actually just the opposite is true, it provides them with freedom and mobility.

While there is not complete agreement among disability advocates, at this time, the common and preferred term is "person with a disability." With this language, the person comes first. Avoid using "the" as it implies "other." Instead of "the handicapped," "the retarded," "the disabled," say a "person with a

physical disability," or "a person with a developmental disability," or "a person who is blind." It is not necessary to mention
a person's disability unless it is relevant to your point. It is considered acceptable to use "disabled person/people" in writing.
The correct term for a person without a disability is "nondisabled."

Preaching

Thoughtful exegesis and preaching of the disability passages
and healing narratives are an important piece in a theology of
access. Because the experiences and perspectives of people with
disabilities are not yet being explored in any comprehensive
way within the theological community, I believe that biblical
scholars, theologians, and pastoral ministers often interpret and
preach the disability passages without regard for the experience
and feelings of the disabled person. For example, those interpreting healing stories need to be mindful of the inherent ten-
sions between literal, more-than-literal, and metaphorical
interpretations. Even the careful and sophisticated biblical
reader tends to move in and out of these three interpretive
modes without realizing it. This process is often harmful to people with disabilities whose experience of embodiment is re-
duced to a metaphor or who are rendered profoundly "other"
by distorted literal translations.

Disability advocate Josie Byzek suggests there are different
ways to interpret and preach the disability Scriptures that do
not foster the oppression of people with disabilities. For example, regarding the story of the healing of the man with paralysis
in Matthew 9: 1–7, she presents an interesting interpretation:

> Jesus made the man whole! Yet when read carefully, it becomes
> clear that the grace Jesus imparted to the man was imparted *be-*
> *fore* the man was cured. Jesus forgave the man's sins *before* he was
> cured. For the man to have his sins forgiven by Jesus would have
> been enough for both of them, neither expressed dissatisfaction

in the text. But then Jesus realized that the scribes thought him a blasphemer for forgiving the man's sins, so he cured the man. Clearly the cure was to make a point: Which is easier to say, "Your sins are forgiven," or to say "Rise and walk"?

Jesus forgave the man's sins in his paralytic state. Jesus saw the man as worthy and deserving of God's love just as every other— nondisabled—person in the room. Not any more or any less "whole." If Jesus did not accept the man for who he was, equal to all other people in the room, then he would have healed the man first and forgiven his sins second.[26]

Consider creative new ways to preach the disability Scriptures. Some suggestions include:

- Do not objectify the disabled person. Instead, focus on their personal qualities or behavior or some other aspect of the story. Never describe the healing in a way that creates pity for the person with the disability.
- Do not reduce a person's experience of embodiment to a metaphor. Everyone has heard the metaphor about spiritual blindness a thousand times anyway!
- Use the disability passages as a way to mention the new paradigms in disability philosophy or disability education.
- Seek the perspective of a person with a disability as you prepare your preaching.
- Be sensitive to pejorative or offensive language in the passages and modify if possible.

"Churchplace Accommodations"

All who are serious about inclusion and allowing Christians with disabilities the opportunity to live out their true vocations need to learn about adaptive equipment,[27] natural supports,[28] and the various types of "high-tech" and "low-tech" assistive technology that are available to help people with disabilities increase, maintain, or improve functional capabilities and live and work independently. These accommodations have the potential to create incredible opportunities for people with disabilities within our church. However revolutionary the concept, we must create "churchplace accommodations"[29] using assistive technology, natural supports, and adaptive equipment to create access for people with disabilities. Widespread use of churchplace accommodations will facilitate the full and active contribution of many great gifts that are currently lost to the church.

Robert R. Williams is a forty-three-year-old man. He has cerebral palsy, very limited speech, and is unable to walk. Twenty years ago, Williams would probably have been institutionalized or, if he were fortunate, live at home with his aging parents. Instead, he was the commissioner for the Administration on Disabilities during the Clinton administration. He set disability policy on the national level, advised the president of the United States on disability issues, oversaw a $109 million dollar budget, and supervised a staff of two hundred. He traveled extensively with a personal assistant and a specially trained dog. Williams uses a computerized voice synthesizer called, most appropriately, a Liberator. He types what he wants to say into the Liberator and it speaks for him. He also uses his Liberator as a computer to generate work and communicate via e-mail. Bob Williams is bright, articulate, severely disabled, and extremely successful because of assistive technology.[30]

A prerequisite for learning, for working, and simply for living in the twenty-first century will be access to communication and telecommunications for everyone, especially people with disabilities. Commissioner Williams speaks of "the deeply transformational properties of this thing we call assistive technology."[31] Conversely, assistive technology can help people with disabilities access the deeply transformational experience of inclusion in the Christian community.

Access to Ministerial Leadership

It is probably for the best that the crucified Jesus did not seek ordination. The limits to his mobility caused by the damage to the tendons and ligaments from the nail wounds in his feet and wrists would have rendered him unsuitable for the job, at least by contemporary standards. He probably would have limped and, even if he were able to manage physically, those scars might have been a "turnoff" to many. This caustic observation is used to make the point that people with disabilities have often been denied access to liturgical leadership. Jan Robitscher recounts her own struggles to become ordained and says, "If it is difficult for persons with disabilities to gain physical and social access to the church, it is nearly impossible, if such persons should feel called by God, to gain access to that process which leads to ordination for liturgical leadership."[32]

In *Called: New Thinking on Christian Vocation*, Basil Pennington says, "The Christian community might have to examine the possibility of certain prejudices existing in her midst that may be impeding some of our fellow Christians from living out their true vocations."[33]

There will never be full inclusion of people with disabilities until every job in the Christian community is open to them. From priest to pope, from deacon to director of religious education, from liturgist to lay reader, people with disabilities must be given the opportunity to serve according to their gifts. Their vocations must be taken seriously. Others in the community must encourage people with disabilities to take on leadership roles, and support them once they are in these roles. Advocate for access to ministerial leadership for people with disabilities. Be knowledgeable about ways to accommodate different disabilities that will remove barriers.

Conclusion

In this section, I have laid out a theology of access that names Jesus as copious host, suggests a relational Christology derived from Jesus in relationship with people with disabilities, proposes the Holy Spirit as a model of inclusion, and calls for the church to be an accessible community. These theologies move from theory and idea to concrete praxis and suggestions. The suggestions for inclusion and access are by no means comprehensive, but are rather a sampling of some of the topics and issues that must be addressed to begin to include people with disabilities. In the final chapter of this book, I develop a disability spirituality centered in friendship and vulnerability.

∼

NINE

Human Vulnerability: Source of Communion in the Kingdom

Giving praise and thanks to you, O God
In whose image we have all been created,
We gather in faith and love,
Where through the power of the Spirit,
all our bodies,
disabled and nondisabled alike,
become one Body in Christ Jesus

With tender mercy and love
you created life and hope
out of darkness and emptiness,
and then in your wisdom,
because you understood that human vulnerability
is the source of communion in the Kingdom,
you sent your only child to enter into the frailty of human life.

Your graciousness is a never-ending source of justice and mercy
best known to us through Jesus, the Christ,
Who in life, death and resurrection,
preached hope and inclusion.

Even when we sin by excluding
those who society pushes to the margins because they are different,
you continue to shower us with mercy by inviting us back to the
table of embodied love,
giving us yet another chance to taste and drink of a justice that welcomes
the estranged and the stranger as friend
and bids us, here and now,
to join you in building the Kingdom.[34]

Beyond Access

If access is to be more than an idea or passing fad, our praxis must take a different direction built on the acknowledgment that human vulnerability is the source of communion in the Kingdom. I am deeply committed to principles of advocacy, social justice, and inclusionary practices. However, my experience has shown me that they are not enough. No laws, bishop's letters, human service paradigms, social programs, or parish accessibility committees will ever truly provide access to people with disabilities. Liberation and real access to the community will only be realized through personal relationships that develop into genuine friendships where shared vulnerability is the rule, not the exception.

Accessibility is not the same thing as hospitality.[35] Reverend Richard Steele explains it well when he says:

> . . . the goal of making facilities more "accessible" will never suffice. Certainly it is a necessary starting point. But unless it is accompanied by a thorough change in those two alternate but equally debilitating attitudes which society generally takes toward its frailest members, heartless indifference and condescending pity, the disabled and their families will remain alienated, and all the renovations made on public buildings will succeed only in making society's "cripples" more visible. . . . What good is it to get into public buildings if you still feel like strangers in a strange land. What good is it to get into public buildings if you still feel like an outsider while you're there?[36]

Catherine LaCugna calls God's household "a domain of inclusiveness, interdependence, and cooperation."[37] Inclusivity, interdependence, and cooperation happen best among people who recognize that human vulnerability is the source of communion in the Kingdom that God desires for us. One of the reasons that it is so important for us to challenge stereotypes of people with disabilities is because these stereotypes make real friendship impossible. As long as we continue to view a person with the disability as "the other," the person we need to "help," cast in the role of "the least," we close off the possibility of friendship and block the way to interdependence.

Don Saliers says that "if 'inclusiveness' is to be more than a slogan, our practice must lead to acknowledgment of our common humanity in the image of God and to the discovery of what it means to be 'present' to one another. Mere affirmation is not enough; rather, upbuilding one another in love is the point. Loving the other and oneself for the sake of God is a profound capacity that requires entering deeply into our common humanity, particularly into the mystery of limit, into joy in the midst of tribulation, and into the discovery of giftedness in difference."[38]

Wolf Wolfensberger is an influential disability professional and advocate. He is one of the architects of contemporary human service models and his work planted the seeds of the community inclusion movement. Wolfensberger uses spiritual metaphors to describe what he thinks is most important, when he says:

> There are many people, especially wounded and handicapped people, who now do not have viable, relatively unconditional one-to-one supportive relationships. If people are no longer willing to engage in those kinds of relationships, laws can be passed, unlimited funds can be allocated—and still nothing will work . . . if individuals, **on a personal basis**, do not bind the wounds of the sick, do not give bread to the hungry, do not console the brokenhearted and visit the imprisoned, do not liberate the captives

of oppression and do not bury the dead, then nothing will work.[39]

As Christian people trying to live the gospel in the modern world, we are called to respond to the challenges of our times. We are called to fight oppression, even at personal cost. We are called to advocate for those who are oppressed, those who find themselves pushed to the margins by a contemporary society that values self-sufficiency and competence. We are called, on a personal basis, to bind, to give, to console, to visit, to bury, and to liberate our brothers and sisters. These holy and timeless actions are what are needed now; indeed, what has always been needed. And most of all, we are called to friendship.

Beyond Access: A Spirituality of Friendship

Lillian Rubin argues that friendship has a very significant place in the "drama of human development"[40] and is absolutely crucial to our well being from early childhood through old age. Paul Wadell believes that "Personhood is a social creation, not an individual one, inasmuch as we come to life through the crucible of friendship, through the love, care and affection given us by others. The more fully we relate in love and trust to others, the more fully we come unto ourselves."[41] In a very real sense, the extent to which we are known and loved by others, and the extent to which we are able to love, is the extent to which we exist.

There are those who would claim that friendship has fallen on hard times in the modern world. In many ways, the notion of friendship, in both the classical and Christian traditions, is at cross-purposes with the values of modernity where there is heavy emphasis placed on individualism. Robert Schrieter names the following concepts as the values of modernity: autonomy, control, freedom, rights (rather than responsibility), and progress.[42] Although these values appeared to create an attractive vision of society, in reality, they are a movement away from authentic friendship. Language about rights, control, and freedom does not foster situations of shared commitment to the common good or any willingness to put others before oneself. Independence, rather than interdependence, is named as the primary virtue.

What qualities are found in authentic friendships? Lawrence S. Cunningham and Keith J. Egan name the following qualities: "Genuine caring for another, attention to their needs, a willingness to listen attentively, a willingness to be vulnerable, a willingness to risk, hospitality, faithfulness, loyalty, trust—and most of all a love that is other-centered."[43] Lillian Rubin, through compiling data from hundreds of interviews, names these qualities: "trust, honesty, respect, commitment, safety, support, generosity, loyalty, mutuality, constancy, understanding and acceptance."[44] Paul Wadell names justice, generosity, compassion, and availability and calls friendship "a moral skill that demands at least minimal generosity and thoughtfulness, a capacity to care, and at least sufficient justice to recognize how we are obligated to respond to the needs and well being of others."[45]

People who are not disabled usually take friendships for granted. Robert Perske, a well-known disability professional and advocate writes about the "pain experienced by people with disabilities when they are deprived of mutually satisfying friendships with ordinary people." In his lovely book, *Circle of Friends*, beautifully illustrated by his wife, Martha, Perske shares stories of simple and extraordinary friendships of disabled and nondisabled people showing how these relationships have enriched their lives. In a chapter entitled "Why Friends Are Important," Perske makes the following observations about the familiar but elusive term friendship. While we need our families, friends help us stretch beyond our families. Friends help us rehearse our adult roles and serve as fresh role models. Sometimes we choose certain friends because we see something in them that we wish for ourselves. Good friendships are a mystery. Friendship is attractive; others watch interactions between friends with great interest. Friendships generate their own energy and are a haven from the stresses of everyday life. Friendships are reciprocal, providing opportunities for giving and taking.[46]

The Perskes tell us that they "found a few down-to-earth, large-hearted adults and students who became good friends with people once thought too limited or strange for life in ordinary neighborhoods. To our surprise, these friendships became our "living documents.""[47] I would go so far as to call these stories "sacramental" documents for they narrate the spirituality of friendship that must characterize a theology of access with staying power.

The story of Judith Snow describes well the spirituality of friendship to which I refer. Judith, a Canadian woman living in Toronto, has muscular dystrophy and uses an electric wheelchair, which she operates with her right thumb—the only part of her body below her neck that she can move. Judith is described as having a "deep, warm voice and a kind round rose-cheeked face and a graciousness and intense love of life."[48] Tenacious and ambitious, Judith graduated from York University with honors and founded and became the first director of the university's Center for Special Services for Students with Disabilities. Although she did the work of two people, she was not paid as much as one nondisabled professional and she could not afford to pay for the attendant care she needed. The book recounts a grim narrative describing her multiple attempts to obtain housing and attendant care and her physical decline to the point of total exhaustion and complete collapse. Judith Snow would have died if not for five people who circled around her forming the Joshua Committee. This circle of friends stepped in and worked untiringly for months to develop a support system for Judith that comprehensively addressed all her needs: attendant care, finances and budgeting, housing, advocacy by confronting the social service system that had let her down, overall coordination, and even a "cheerleader" to keep the group's morale up! When she was strong enough, Judith herself became the sixth member of this circle of friends where she was encouraged to take control of her own support system as soon as she was able. The group allowed Judith a space where she could be heard and where she could cry and scream. This group of friends held the "quiet, intuitive belief that five persons together could mysteriously generate a power much more than each of the five separately."[49] Today, Judith is recognized as a leading expert on the political and social situation of people with disabilities. She calls herself a "portable visionary who tries to show others how to encircle a person in crisis."[50] The Joshua Committee still meets, mostly for social reasons, and Judith now has many circles of friends beyond the five members of the Joshua Committee. In Judith's community over a hundred other circles of friends have been documented as a result of this group. Judith's circle of friends moved her toward community in a very particular way, for several years later she married a man she met at an advocacy meeting.

Friendship moves us away from self-absorption, beyond ourselves, toward community, giving us the courage and the freedom to seek the lonely other. Friendship encourages openness, generosity, graciousness, and hospitality, and ultimately leads to vulnerability, the source of communion in the Kingdom. I am told that Jürgen Moltmann, the great theologian known for his theology of hope, has a brother with disabilities. He certainly writes about the topic of disability as if he does, for he understands that human vulnerability is the source of communion in the Kingdom. He says, "The eternal God took on not only the limited and mortal aspects of humanity. . . . He took on our disabilities and made them a part of his eternal life. He takes on our tears and makes them an expression of his own pain."[51] The great paradox of the Paschal Mystery is that human vulnerability is the source of communion in the Kingdom. Our route to union with God and with each other is through the sharing of our joys, our tears, our pain, our limitations, and our hopes.

Beyond Friendship: Communion

Devoted God,
again and again,
you lead your people from chaos to covenant
reminding our ancestors that your passion for
our holy freedom never wavers.

When the time for the new and final covenant arrived
your divine vulnerability graced the earth
and your Word was made flesh and
dwelt among us
showing us how to live in your love and
to care for each other.
Recalling with gratitude
how your Spirit has transfigured our lives
we profess our faith in the salvation poured out for us in
your Son, our Lord, Jesus Christ.

On the night before his utter vulnerability was revealed
He sat together in a circle of friendship
with his brothers and sisters to explain
the simple way he wished to be remembered
from that day forward.

He took table bread,
gave you thanks and praise
and broke the bread saying:
"Take this all of you and eat it,
this is my Body which will be given up for you."

He took a cup filled with table wine,
giving you praise and thanks saying:
"Take this all of you and drink from it,
this cup is my blood, the blood of the
new and everlasting covenant.
It will be shed for you and for all so
sins may be forgiven.
Do this in memory of me."

Recalling Jesus
who was friend to people with disabilities
all through his life,

Recalling Jesus
and the gaping wounds in his hands and feet
at the time of his death, and

Recalling the Risen Christ
who showed his disabled body without shame,

We offer you, our Creator,
these gifts of bread and wine
and we ask that your Spirit which rests on these gifts,
descend on and hover around this community
so that we may learn to be Christ to one another.[52]

My brother Bobby died on a Saturday in June. He was twenty-two years old. I had just returned home from a one-week business trip to Europe with my husband. I had nervously accompanied him, not really wanting to go, as I was anxious about leaving Bobby who was growing weaker and was increasingly less able to tolerate his dialysis treatments. I am pretty sure he waited to die until I came home. I got home late Friday evening and made my way up to see him early Saturday morning. He was in his bed waiting for me. His first question was "What did you bring me?" After examining his gifts, which included a funky pair of boxer shorts with matching slippers, he wanted to "talk turkey." I am sure he had tried to pursue a serious conversation about his approaching death with our father, but my dear father couldn't bring himself to it. Bobby was serious and direct. He first wanted to be sure about where he would die. He made it clear that he did not want to die in a hospital . . . "no tubes," he told me. I promised him he would die at home. He then wanted to know where he would be buried . . . "in the coffin, in the graveyard, right?" "Yes," I told him, "in the graveyard, in a coffin." Making the transition from the graveyard to heaven, he asked me, "I see Jesus in heaven?" I nodded my head. "I see our mother in heaven, right?" "Yes," I told him, "We believe mother will be waiting for you and you will be very happy to see each other." I will never forget his next question. "Is there Radio Shack in heaven?" Radio Shack was his favorite store, and our father who totally spoiled him was always buying and replacing his favorite gadgets—a pair of walkie-talkies, a CB Radio, or a portable radio with a headset. "Yes, they have a big Radio Shack in heaven." He smiled, pleased at this news. Then a moment later, he got a worried look on his face. "Who gonna give me money in heaven?" He was obviously remembering and referring to the fact that our mother was much stricter than our father and was far less likely to indulge him at Radio Shack. I thought for a moment and then said, "In heaven, Radio Shack is free." This seemed to please and satisfy him, and he told me to go and get him some Gatorade. When I came back five minutes later with his drink, he was gone. We buried him next to our mother two days later.

Literally hundreds of people, too diverse to ever describe, reached out to Bobby during his seventeen years with our family. We sent out a thank-you card to the many people who were so kind to him during his life, and so kind to our family when he died. In this card we wrote,

> There was no one like Bobby. He had unique, intangible qualities that made him so appealing. Bobby was a paradox. He was retarded, yet he was clever. He had strange features, big ears and crooked limbs, and yet he was beautiful. He was aggressive yet gentle. He was self-centered, yet generous. He could be really bad, yet he was an angel. And he was ours. We loved him, and yet he loved us more than we loved him. We gave him everything we could, and yet he gave us more than we gave him.

Bobby taught us patience, perseverance, tolerance, and unselfishness, and because of him we were showered with the holy gifts of joy, frustration, despair, and intense love. During his short life, Bobby presided as the copious host of our family. I believe he presides still, seated next to my mother, and my husband, and the saints and angels, and all the holy men and women who have gone before us.

In the introduction to this book I said that I hoped that I would be able to convince you that access is both a moral and a mystical matter, and that inclusion of people with disabilities is a mandate of the Christian life. I hope my arguments have been convincing. I hope that I have been loyal to the disability community, and I hope that my theological reflection resonates with the religious community. I hope that I have inspired some of you to be copious hosts. And, finally, I hope there is a big, well-stocked, free Radio Shack in heaven.

Notes

The reader should be aware that there are three different disability publications with similar names: (1) *The Disability Rag and Resource*, a bimonthly publication in a magazine/newspaper format, which changed its name in the mid-90s to (2) *The Ragged Edge*, and (3) the 1994 book edited by Barrett Shaw and entitled *The Ragged Edge: The Disability Experience from the First Fifteen Years of the Disability Rag*. Shortened references to the book will include the rubric "ed. Shaw."

Introduction

1. Rahner's notion of the mysticism of everyday life is well explained in chapter 3 of Michael Skelley's *The Liturgy of the World: Karl Rahner's Theology of Worship* (Collegeville, Minn.: Liturgical Press, 1991).

2. David Tracy, *Blessed Rage for Order: The New Pluralism in Theology* (New York: Seabury Press, 1975), 43–45.

3. See chapter 5 for a description of this concept.

4. Joseph P. Shapiro, *No Pity: People with Disabilities Forging a New Civil Rights Movement* (New York: Random House, 1994), 5.

5. Nancy Mairs, "Learning from Suffering," *Christian Century*, 6 May 1998, 481.

6. Nancy L. Eiesland, "Barriers and Bridges: Relating the Disability Rights Movement and Religious Organizations," in *Human Disability and the Service of God: Reassessing Religious Practice*, ed. Nancy L. Eiesland and Don E. Saliers (Nashville, Tenn.: Abingdon Press, 1998), 200.

7. Ibid., 201.

8. Tracy, *Blessed Rage for Order*, 32.

9. Ibid., 45.

10. Ibid., 49.

11. Eiesland, "Barriers and Bridges," 20.

12. James F. Keenan, S.J., "Ten Reasons Why Thomas Is Important Today," *New Black Friars* 75 (1994): 357.

Part I: The Contemporary Disability Movement

1. Alan Gartner and Tom Joe, eds., *Images of the Disabled, Disabling Images* (New York: Praeger Publishers, 1987), 207; quoted in Deborah Creamer, "Finding God in Our Bodies, Part I," *Journal of Religion in Disability and Rehabilitation* 2, no. 2 (1995): 33.

2. Americans with Disabilities Act, *Statues at Large*, S. 993 (1990).

3. Pope John Paul II, "Address to the International Conference on the Concerns of Persons with Disabilities," Vatican City, October 1988.

4. See Susan Wendell's book, *The Rejected Body: Feminist Philosophical Reflections on Disability* (New York and London: Routledge, 1996), for an excellent treatment of this topic.

5. Joseph P. Shapiro, *No Pity: People with Disabilities Forging a New Civil Rights Movement* (New York: Random House, 1994), 7.

6. Ibid., 11.

7. Nancy L. Eiesland, *The Disabled God: Toward a Liberatory Theory of Disability* (Nashville, Tenn.: Abingdon Press, 1994), 27.

8. Janet Miller Rife and Ginny Thornburgh, *From Barriers to Bridges: A Community Action Guide for Congregations and People with Disabilities* (Washington, D.C.: National Organization on Disability, 1996), 50.

9. Susan Wendell, "Towards a Feminist Theology of Disability," *Hypatia* 4, no. 2 (Summer 1989): 75.

10. Americans with Disabilities Act, *Statues at Large*, S. 993 (1990).

11. Al Condeluci, *Interdependence: The Route to Community* (Winter Park, Fla.: PMD Publishers Group, 1991), 35–36.

12. Wendell, *The Rejected Body*, 14.

13. Ibid., 16.

14. Charles Gourney, "Disability and Destiny," *Journal of Religion in Disability and Rehabilitation* 2, no. 1 (1995): 74.

15. Barbara J. Blodgett, "Graced Vulnerability," *Journal of Religion in Disability and Rehabilitation* 2, no. 3 (1995): 75.

16. Andrew Solomon, "Deaf Is Beautiful, *New York Times Magazine,* 28 August 1994, 67.

17. Dennis D. Schurter, "Jesus' Ministry with People with Disabilities: Scriptural Foundations for Churches' Inclusive Ministry," *Journal of Religion in Disability and Rehabilitation* 1, no. 4 (1994): 47.

18. Charles Gourney, "Making Our Hearts Accessible, Too," *Journal of Religion in Disability and Rehabilitation* 2, no. 3 (1995): 4.

19. Ibid.

20. Shapiro, *No Pity,* 106.

21. Americans with Disabilities Act, *Statutes at Large,* S. 933 (1990).

22. Metz developed the idea of the dangerous memory in the context of the narrative of Jesus' life in *Faith in History and Society* (New York: Crossroad, 1980).

23. Estimates of disabled people exterminated in Nazi Germany range from two hundred thousand to one million. More detailed information about this can be found in Martha Russell, *Beyond Ramps: Disability at the End of the Social Contract* (Monroe, Me.: Common Courage Press, 1998); Shapiro, *No Pity;* and in Wolf Wolfensberger, "The Extermination of Handicapped People in World War II Germany," *Mental Retardation* 19, no. 1 (1981): 1–7.

24. Not Dead Yet is an organization of disability activists that formed in April 1996 to oppose the legalization of assisted suicide as the ultimate form of disability discrimination.

25. Shapiro, *No Pity,* 161.

26. Lisa Blumberg, "Public Stripping," *The Ragged Edge: The Disability Experience from the Pages of the First Fifteen Years of the Disability Rag,* ed. Barrett Shaw (Louisville, Ky.: Avocado Press, 1994), 73–78.

27. Edward L. Hooper, "The Room of Pain and Loneliness," in *The Ragged Edge,* ed. Shaw, 55.

28. Ibid., 56.

29. Ibid., 57

30. R. C. Smith, "An Audience for Amy," *The Ragged Edge,* May/June 1998, 31.

31. Condeluci, *Interdependence,* 16.

32. Ibid., 18.

33. From a Disability and Oppression Workshop conducted by D. Ploof and L. Spruill, Pittsburgh, Penn., 1990.

34. Joseph Shapiro, "Disability Policy and the Media: A Stealth Civil Rights Movement Bypasses the Press and Defies Conventional Wisdom," *Policy Studies Journal* 22, no. 1 (1994): 123.

35. Wolf Wolfensberger, *The Principle of Normalization in Human Services* (Toronto: National Institute on Mental Health, 1972), 15.

36. Charles Gourney, "Faith, Despair and Disability," *Journal of Religion in Disability and Rehabilitation* 1, no. 3 (1994): 22.

37. Mary Stainton, "Healing Stories: Critiquing Old and Creating New," *Journal of Religion in Disability and Rehabilitation* 2, no. 4 (1994): 68.

38. Gourney, "Disability and Destiny," 75.

39. Deborah Creamer, "Finding God in Our Bodies: Theology from the Perspective of People with Disabilities, Part II," *Journal of Religion in Disability and Rehabilitation* 2, no. 2 (1995): 68.

40. Letter to author, 8 August 1998.

41. Rife and Thornburgh, *From Bridges to Barriers*, 4.

42. Ibid.

43. This term came into use after publication of an article entitled "Disconfirmation" by Billy Golfus, in *The Ragged Edge*, ed. Shaw. Golfus describes his experience of being rendered invisible after a head injury. He writes that this is a common experience for newly disabled people, who often tell of their old friends acting like they no longer exist.

44. Wolfensberger, *The Principle of Normalization*, 16.

45. Ibid., 19.

46. Ibid., 20.

47. Ibid., 22.

48. Ibid., 23.

49. Ibid., 23–24.

50. Ibid., 21–22.

51. John 9:1–6.

52. This topic is treated in greater length in chapter 5.

53. Matthew 25:31–46.

54. Pope John Paul II, "Address to the International Conference on the Concerns of Persons with Disabilities," Vatican City, October 1988.

55. There are those who would argue that there is a hierarchy within the disability community based on the type of disability. While this might be true in terms of external perceptions and in resource al-

locations, within the disability movement itself this hierarchy is less significant. See James I. Charlton, *Nothing About Us Without Us: Disability Oppression and Empowerment* (Berkeley: University of California Press, 1998) for a discussion on this topic.

56. Harrison Rainie and Kata Hetter, "The Most Lasting Kennedy Legacy," *U.S. News and World Report*, 15 November 1993.

57. From a speech by Ed Roberts; text provided by Colleen Wieck and the Minnesota Disabilities Planning Council.

58. Ibid.

59. Ibid.

60. Ibid.

61. Unless otherwise noted, the primary source for the information in this section is Fred Polka, *The ABC-CLIO Companion to the Disability Rights Movement* (Santa Barbara, Calif.: ABC-CLIO, 1997).

62. Ibid.

63. Condeluci, *Independence*, 150–57.

64. Robert Perske, "The Dignity of Risk," *Mental Retardation* 10, no. 1 (1972).

65. Paul Longmore, "The Second Phase: From Disability Rights to Disability Culture," *The Disability Rag and Resource*, September/October 1995, 4.

66. Cheryl Marie Wade, "Disability Culture Rap," *The Disability Rag and Resource*, September/October 1992, 37.

67. Laura Hershey, "Pride," *The Disability Rag and Resource*, July/August 1991, 1, 4–5.

68. Shapiro, *No Pity*, 14.

Part II: Reinterpreting the Christian Tradition from a Disability Perspective

1. This is a selective list of topics. There are numerous other Christian "texts" and theological topics that could also be considered from a disability perspective. Some examples of these topics may be found in Nancy Eiesland and Don Saliers, eds., *Human Disability and the Service of God: Reassessing Religious Practice* (Nashville, Tenn.: Abingdon, 1998), and in a variety of articles in the *Journal of Religion in Disability and Rahabilitation*.

2. Barrett Shaw, ed., *The Ragged Edge: The Disability Experience from the Pages of the First Fifteen Years of the Disability Rag* (Louisville, Ky.: Avocado Press, 1994), xii.

3. Beldon Lane, "Grace and the Grotesque," *Christian Century* 107, no. 33 (14 November 1990): 1069.

4. Ibid.

5. *Is Christ Disabled? A Study Guide on Disability* (Chicago: Campus Ministry Communications, 1981), 25.

6. Susan A. Ross, "God's Embodiment and Women," in *Freeing Theology: The Essentials of Theology in Feminist Perspective*, ed. Catherine Mowry LaCugna (San Francisco: HarperCollins, 1993), 195.

7. Ibid.

8. Barbara A. B. Patterson, "Redeemed Bodies: Fullness of Life," in *Human Disability and the Service of God*, 103.

9. Ibid., 127.

10. Ibid.

11. Ibid., 128.

12. Lane, "Grace and the Grotesque," 1068.

13. Ibid., 1069.

14. "Press Conference on the Release of the United Nations' Report 'Human Rights and Disabled Persons,' " *Chicago Tribune*, 5 December 1993.

15. James I. Charlton, *Nothing About Us Without Us: Disability Oppression and Empowerment* (Berkeley: University of California Press, 1998), 21.

16. Gustavo Gutierrez, "Liberation Theology," in *The New Dictionary of Social Thought*, ed. Judith A. Dwyer (Collegeville, Minn.: Liturgical Press, 1994), 548–53.

17. Ibid.

18. Juan Luis Segondo, *The Liberation of Theology*, trans. John Drury (Maryknoll, N.Y.: Orbis Books, 1976), 7–9.

19. Ibid.

20. "Hermeneutics" is a popular term used in theological work to describe the science and art of interpretation. The phrase "hermeneutic of suspicion" is used when one wants to bring a motive or outcome of a particular interpretation into question.

21. "Ableist" is a term that disability activists are attempting to bring into use. The word has approximately the same meaning as rac-

ist, sexist, or heterosexist. It is telling that there is no commonly accepted language for describing the way people with disabilities are oppressed.

22. With thanks to my good friend Wayne Cavalier, O.P., for very helpful conversations and insights on this topic.

23. The scope of this work does not permit an examination of the disability passages in the Hebrew Scriptures and the Pauline letters. However, this would be a valuable project.

24. Colleen C. Grant, "Reinterpreting the Healing Narratives," in *Human Disability and the Service of God*, 76–77.

25. Ginny Thornburgh, ed., *Loving Justice: The ADA and the Religious Community* (Washington, D.C.: National Organization on Disability, 1995), 4.

26. The pronoun "he" is used here because all of the disabled people in the Gospels, except one, are men.

27. *A New Way of Thinking* is the title of a publication from the Minnesota Developmental Disabilities Planning Council, which became a popular phrase in the disability movement.

28. S.v. "cure," *The American Heritage Dictionary*, Second College Edition, 1982.

29. S.v. "heal," ibid.

30. See Matthew 4:24; 15:29–31; 21:14; and Luke 7:21. The other group stories mention the curing of diseases and illnesses, not disabilities.

31. This story bears similarities to the story in John 4:46–54, although there is no mention of a disability in the account in John's Gospel.

32. Some Scripture commentaries indicate that Bartimaeus is the same person in the stories in Matthew and Luke. As the method of healing differs, I assign them as two people.

33. Josie Byzek, "Jesus and the Paralytic, the Blind, and the Lame: A Sermon," *The Ragged Edge*, November/December 2000, 25.

34. John 5:1–15.

35. Mark 2:12.

36. Matthew 7:37.

37. Matthew 9:33.

38. Matthew 9:2.

39. Byzek, "Jesus and the Paralytic," 23.

40. Eiesland, "Barriers and Bridges," in *Human Disability and the Service of God*, 218.

41. Ibid.

42. Luke 24:39–40.

43. John 20:27.

44. Francis J. Moloney, *The Gospel of John* (Collegeville, Minn.: Liturgical Press, 1998), 290.

45. Gerald S. Sloyan, *John* (Atlanta, Ga.: John Knox Press, 1987), 115.

46. Arthur John Gossip, "The Gospel according to St. John," *The Interpreter's Bible*, vol. 7 (Nashville and New York: Abingdon Press, 1966), 612.

47. Raymond Brown, *The Gospel according to John* (Garden City, N.Y.: Doubleday, 1966), 337.

48. Grant, "Reinterpreting the Healing Narratives," 79.

49. Rudolf Bultmann, *The Gospel of John: A Commentary*, trans. G. R. Beasley-Murray (Philadelphia: Westminster Press, 1971), 238.

50. Giles Hibbert, "John," *Scripture Discussion Commentary* 9, ed. Lawrence Bright (Chicago: ACTA Foundation, 1972), 102.

51. Janet Miller Rife and Ginny Thornburgh, *From Barriers to Bridge: A Community Action Guide for Congregations and People with Disabilities* (Washington, D.C.: National Organization on Disability, 1996), 50.

52. Don Saliers, "Towards a Spirituality of Inclusiveness," in *Human Disability and the Service of God*, 27.

53. Ibid., 20.

54. Gordon W. Lathrop, *Holy Things: A Liturgical Theology* (Minneapolis: Fortress Press, 1993), 90.

55. Ibid., 113.

56. Edward Foley, ed., *Developmental Disabilities and Sacramental Access* (Collegeville, Minn.: Liturgical Press, 1994), 5.

57. Ibid., 11.

58. "Constitution on the Sacred Liturgy," *Sacrosanctum Concilium*, 10.

59. Ibid., 7.

60. Ibid., 14.

61. Nathan Mitchell, "Plenty Good Room: The Dignity of the Assembly," *Worship* 70 (January 1996): 67.

62. Nathan Mitchell, *Cult and Controversy: The Worship of the Eucharist outside the Mass* (Collegeville, Minn.: Liturgical Press, 1982), 8.

63. Foley, *Developmental Disabilities and Sacramental Access*, 9.

64. With thanks to Pam Neumann for this phrase.

65. Deborah Creamer, "Finding God in Our Bodies: Theology from the Perspective of People with Disabilities, Part I," *Journal of Religion in Disability and Rehabilitation* 2, no. 1 (1995): 34.

66. Lathrop, *Holy Things*, 119.

67. John Sachs, "Holy Spirit in Christian Worship," in *The New Dictionary of Sacramental Worship*, ed. Peter Fink (Collegeville, Minn.: Liturgical Press, 1990), 536.

68. Lathrop, *Holy Things*, 114–15.

69. Mitchell, "Plenty Good Room," 65.

70. Lathrop, *Holy Things*, 119.

Part III: A Theology of Access

1. Catherine Mowry LaCugna, *God for Us: The Trinity and Christian Life* (New York: HarperSanFrancisco, 1991), 388.

2. Edward Schilleeckx, *Jesus: An Experiment in Christology*, trans. Hubert Hoskins (New York: Seabury Press, 1979), 213.

3. Ibid., 218.

4. LaCugna, *God for Us*, 377–411.

5. Ibid., 400.

6. Ibid.

7. C. S. Mann, *Mark: A New Translation with Introduction and Commentary* (Garden City, N.Y.: Doubleday, 1986), 422.

8. Ibid., 594.

9. Ibid., 421.

10. Jacques Dupont, "Blind Bartimaeus (Mark 10:46–52)," *Theology Digest* 33, no. 2 (Summer 1996): 228.

11. Ibid., 226.

12. Robert Grundy, *Mark: A Commentary on His Apology for the Cross* (Grand Rapids, Mich.: William. Eerdmans, 1993), 595.

13. Dupont, "Blind Bartimaeus," 226.

14. Reynolds Price, Foreword to David Rhoads and Donald Michie, *Mark's Story: An Introduction to the Narrative of a Gospel* (Philadelphia: Fortress Press, 1982), 3.

15. Robert Schreiter, class lecture, Boston College, 2 August 1996.

16. Elizabeth A. Johnson, *Woman, Earth, and Creator Spirit* (New York: Paulist Press, 1993), 19.

17. Ibid., 20.

18. See definition and description in chapter 5.

19. *Theological Dictionary of the New Testament,* ed. Gerhard Kittel (Grand Rapids, Mich.: Eerdmans, 1985), 779.

20. D. Bruce Woll, *Johannine Christology in Conflict: Authority, Rank, and Succession in the First Farewell Discourse* (Chico, Calif.: Scholars Press, 1981), 80–81.

21. Elizabeth A. Johnson, *She Who Is: The Mystery of God in Feminist Theological Discourse* (New York: Crossroad, 1996), 132.

22. Ibid., 127.

23. This phrase is borrowed from the title of James I. Charlton's book *Nothing About Us Without Us* (Berkeley: University of California Press, 1998).

24. Jennie Weiss Block, *Project Neighborhood: Community Living Alternatives for People with Developmental Disabilities* (Tallahassee, Fla.: Florida Developmental Disabilities Council, 1989), 1.

25. Jan B. Robitscher, "Through Glasses Darkly: Discovering a Liturgical Place," in *Human Disability and the Service of God: Reassessing Religious Practice,* ed. Nancy L. Eiesland and Don E. Saliers (Nashville, Tenn.: Abingdon Press, 1998), 148.

26. Josie Byzek, "Jesus and the Paralytic, the Blind, and the Lame: A Sermon," *The Ragged Edge,* November/December 2000, 23.

27. Adaptive equipment refers to adaptations that can be made to equipment to facilitate independence. Usually simple, these might include a voice-activated light switch, adapted clothing, modified eating utensils and writing equipment, a lowered desk or seating and positioning systems.

28. Natural supports refer to things a person with a disability might need to function as independently as possible within natural and age-appropriate settings. These might include an electric wheelchair, a job, and transportation.

29. Borrowing from disability language, this is an adapted use of the terms "workplace accommodations" and "reasonable accommodations," two key principles in disability culture.

30. Some might question the cost of the accommodations Mr. Williams uses; however, the cost of maintaining his care in an institution

would be far greater, and no price can be put on the loss that is suffered should his talents and gifts not be used.

31. Robert R. Williams, "Assistive Technology Exceeding All Expectations," *Assistive Technology Quarterly* 5, nos. 2, 3, and 4.

32. Robitscher, "Through Glasses Darkly," 153.

33. M. Basil Pennington, O.C.S.O., *Called: New Thinking on Christian Vocation* (Minneapolis, Minn.: Seabury Press, 1983), 41.

34. This is the preface from a "Eucharistic Prayer of Inclusion" I wrote that was published in *Ministry and Liturgy* 25, no. 5 (June-July 2000), 15. It was written in memory of Lorette Piper, R.S.C.J.

35. This concept is taken from a footnote in Richard B. Steele's article "Accessibility or Hospitality? Reflections and Experiences of a Father and Theologian," *Journal of Religion in Disability and Rehabilitation* 1, no. 1 (1994). Dr. Steele writes: "I am indebted to Fr. Paul J. Wadell, C.P., associate professor of ethics at the Catholic Theological Union in Chicago, for helping clarify the distinction between accessibility and hospitality, and more generally, for helping me to see how, in modern liberal democratic society, talk about the 'rights' of the disabled can fool people into thinking that they have given them their due while still keeping them at arm's length."

36. Steele, "Accessibility or Hospitality?" 21.

37. LaCugna, *God for Us*, 402.

38. Don E. Saliers, "Towards a Spirituality of Inclusiveness," in *Human Disability and the Service of God*, 29.

39. Wolf Wolfensberger, *A Multi-Component for Advocacy/Protection Schema* (Toronto: Canadian Association for the Mentally Retarded, 1977), 66.

40. Lillian B. Rubin, *Just Friends: The Role of Friendship in Our Lives* (New York: Harper and Row, 1985), 7.

41. Paul J. Wadell, C.P., *The Primacy of Love: An Introduction to the Ethics of Thomas Aquinas* (New York: Paulist Press, 1992), 55.

42. Robert Schreiter, class lecture, Boston College, 24 July 1996.

43. Lawrence S. Cunningham and Keith J. Egan, *Christian Spirituality: Themes from the Tradition* (New York: Paulist Press, 1996), 178.

44. Rubin, *Just Friends*, 7.

45. Paul J. Wadell, C.P., "Growing together in the Divine Love: The Role of Charity in the Moral Theology of Thomas Aquinas," in *Aquinas and Empowerment: Classical Ethics for Ordinary Lives*, ed. G. Simon Herak (Washington, D.C.: Georgetown University Press, 1996), 136.

46. Ibid., 12–13.

47. Robert Perske, *Circle of Friends* (Nashville, Tenn.: Abingdon Press, 1988), 10.

48. Ibid., 15.

49. Ibid., 17.

50. Ibid., 18.

51. Jürgen Moltmann, "Liberating Yourself by Accepting One Another," in *Human Disability and the Service of God,* 116.

52. This is from my "Eucharistic Prayer of Inclusion" referenced in note 34 above.

~

Resource List

Books and Publications

The following is a partial list of books and publications related to the topic of disability and religion from a variety of perspectives. I have read all of the books and publications listed below, and while I am not always in full agreement with the point of view expressed, I can recommend these books and publications as excellent resources for further exploring the relationship between disability and Christianity.

Benton, Janice LaLonde, and Mary Jane Owen. *Opening Doors to People with Disabilities*, volumes 1 and 2. Washington, D.C.: National Catholic Office for Persons with Disabilities, 1995.

Black, Kathy. *A Healing Homiletic: Preaching and Disability*. Nashville: Abingdon Press, 1996.

Browne, Elizabeth J. *The Disabled Disciple: Ministering in a Church Without Barriers*. Liguori, Missouri: Ligouri Publications, 1997.

Eiesland, Nancy L. *The Disabled God: Towards a Liberatory Theology of Disability*. Nashville: Abingdon Press, 1994.

————, and Don E. Saliers, editors. *Human Disability and the Service of God: Reassessing Religious Practice*. Nashville: Abingdon Press, 1998.

Foley, Edward, O.S.F., editor. *Developmental Disabilities and Sac-*

ramental Access. Chicago: Archdiocesan Office of Divine Worship, 1994.

Rife, Janet Miller, and Ginny Thornburgh. *From Barriers to Bridges: A Community Action Guide for Congregations and People with Disabilities.* Washington, D.C.: National Organization on Disability, 1989.

Thornburgh, Ginny, ed. *Loving Justice: The ADA and the Religious Community.* Washington, D.C.: National Organization on Disability, 1995.

———. *From Barriers to Bridges: A Community Action Guide for Congregations and People with Disabilities.* Washington, D.C.: National Organization on Disability, 1996.

United States Conference of Catholic Bishops. *Celebrate and Challenge: On the Ten-Year Anniversary of the Pastoral Statement on People with Disabilities.* Washington, D.C.: 1988.

———. *Guidelines for the Celebration of the Sacraments with Persons with Disabilities.* Washington, D.C.: 1995.

———. *Pastoral Statement of U.S. Catholic Bishops on Persons with Disabilities.* Washington, D.C.: 1978.

Vanier, Jean. *Do Not Be Afraid.* New York: Paulist Press, 1975.

———. *The Broken Body: Journey to Wholeness.* New York: Paulist Press, 1988.

———. *Community and Growth.* New York: Paulist Press, 1979.

Webb-Mitchell, Brent. *Dancing with Disabilities: Opening the Church to All God's Children.* Cleveland: United Church Press, 1996.

———. *God Plays Piano, Too: The Spiritual Lives of Disabled Children,* New York: Crossroad, 1993.

———. *Unexpected Guests at God's Banquet: Welcoming People with Disabilities into the Church.* New York: Crossroad, 1994.

Denominational Resources

The following is a partial list of denominational resources that have specific offices or programs that work toward the inclusion of people with disabilities on the national level. All of these organizations welcome inquiries and many have excellent materials available. Many have local organizations in different cities throughout the United States. Again, while I do not necessarily agree philosophically or practically with all of their positions or practices, these are resources that can be helpful. All information was correct at time of publication.

American Association on Mental Retardation
444 N. Capital Street, N.W., Suite 846
Washington, D.C. 20001-1512
800-424-3688
Religion and Spirituality Division
Vanessa Ervin, President
vj.ervin@att.net

Bethesda Lutheran Home
National Christian Resource Center
700 Hoffman Drive
Watertown, Wisconsin 53094
800-383-8743
920-261-3050
http://www.blhs.org

Christian Council for Persons with Disabilities
7120 W. Dove Court
Milwaukee, Wisconsin 53223
414-357-6672
http://www.ccpd.org
847-742-5100

Episcopal Disability Network
(formerly Task Force on Accessibility)
3024 East Minnehaha Parkway
Minneapolis, Minnesota 55406
888-422-0320, pin # 6634 (toll free): 612-729-1645
http://www.edn4ministry.org disability99@earthlink.net

Evangelical Lutheran Church in America
Disability Ministries Office
8765 W. Higgins Road
Chicago, Illinois 60631
800-638-3522
http://www.elca.org/dis/disability

Institute of Pastoral Initiatives
(formerly: Center on Ministry with Disabled People)
Network on Inclusive Catholic Educators
University of Dayton
300 College Park Drive
Dayton, Ohio 45469-0317
937-229-4325
888.532.3389
pat.carter@notes.udayton.edu

International Jewish Vocational Services
1845 Walnut Street, Suite 640
Philadelphia, Pennsylvania, 19103
215.854.0233
http://www.iajvs.org

Mennonite Mutual Aid Advocacy Department
P.O. Box 483
Goshen, Indiana 46527
800-348-7468
219-533-5344

National Apostolate for Inclusion Ministry
(formerly National Apostolate with Persons with Mental
Retardation)
P.O. Box 218
Riverdale, Maryland 20738-0218
301-699-9500
800-736-1280
http://www.nafim.org

National Catholic Office for Persons with Disabilities (NCPD)
PO Box 29113
Washington, D.C. 20017
202-529-2933 (V/TDD)
http://www.ncpd.org

National Council of Churches
Division of Education and Ministry
Disabilities Ministries
475 Riverside Drive, Room 834
New York, NY 10115
212-870-2673
jleonard@ncccusa.org

National Organization on Disability
Religion and Disability Program
910 16th Street, N.W., Suite 600
Washington, D.C. 20006
202-293-5960
202-293-5968 TDD
800-248-ABLE (2253)